THE PSALMS

OF THE

OLD TESTAMENT

JOHN METCALFE

THE PSALMS

OF THE

OLD TESTAMENT

IN METRE

ACCORDING TO

THE AUTHORISED VERSION

JOHN METCALFE

THE PUBLISHING TRUST
Church Road, Tylers Green, Penn, Buckinghamshire.

—

Printed and Published by
The Publishing Trust
Church Road, Tylers Green
Penn, Buckinghamshire

—

First published January 1985

—

ISBN 0 9506366 7 3

—

Recommended Price £2.50

—

Contents

Contents

THE SINGING OF THE PSALMS

◆◆

TO those unused to singing psalms, the psalter presents a daunting prospect. Not only the book itself, but many of the individual psalms, may at first appear so long that it will seem difficult to know how to begin singing.

To assist the beginner, we have given a short working list of suggested portions in the form of an index at the conclusion of the book. Once these are attempted and mastered, so great will be found the blessing that attends the path of obedience in the singing of psalms, that nothing will stop the delighted singer from going on to possess the whole of this wonderful heritage. Soon even such long psalms as eighteen or seventy-eight might be attempted, for a way will be found in which quite naturally they divide into suitable portions.

In congregational worship, when in the meetings of the saints spiritual subjects are brought before the heart of those assembled, then harmonious passages from the psalms will spontaneously spring to mind to support and enhance the worship with singing. Should this be from a longer psalm, experience will soon teach a kind of flexibility whereby the appropriate context is extracted, with perhaps a suitable verse or two from the beginning and end of the psalm to give fuller expression.

No more than a little perseverance in following these simple suggestions will cause the first tentative steps to give place to the sure movements of experience, and this will be found to yield abundant fruitfulness to those who sing to the LORD a new song.

In both private and family worship, nothing can equal the incalculable benefit of singing steadily and consistently through the whole book of the psalms. Places suggest themselves as to where to break off for that morning or evening in the longer psalms — just as when reading the Bible — and it is simplicity itself to resume singing at the same place on the next occasion.

The use of the psalms in congregational, family and private worship has been the practice of the people of God from the beginning. The Lord Jesus sung psalms, and so did the disciples. The apostles of our Lord and Saviour Jesus Christ commended and commanded this practice in the Gentile churches, laying the foundation of obedient worship throughout the Christian dispensation.

The Lord Jesus Christ himself is said to sing psalms in the midst of his brethren, yea, 'In the midst of the church will I sing praise unto thee.' Thus he quotes the psalm from which he sings, and promises by the inward Spirit to accompany the worshippers from the glory throughout the age. But how can this come to pass, if in modern times we on our part allow the singing of these psalms to lapse? But I trust we shall be found among the faithful remnant that continues steadfast to the end, fulfilling the word of God:

'Speaking to yourselves in psalms and hymns and spiritual songs,' Ephesians 5:19;

and 'Admonishing one another in psalms and hymns and spiritual songs,' Colossians 3:16.

For 'If that which ye have heard from the beginning shall remain in you, ye also shall continue in the Son, and in the Father,' I John 2:24.

★

Finally a word about the great Scottish Psalter, without peer in the gravity and weightiness of its language. Nevertheless it is a fact that, because of its recognised flaws in rhythm and rhyme, and, much more serious, its verbal inaccuracies, several revisions have been attempted over the generations since its first publication.

Yet surely this great work should have been allowed to stand upon its own merit, 'warts and all'. The more so because none of those who have tinkered with it has produced a revision of commensurate weight with the original, and hence their tinkering has made the fault appear far worse, the psalter as a whole having been diminished by the attempt.

The truth is, there is no real alternative but to do the entire work again from the original scriptures. That this is warranted can easily be shown from a list of the graver faults in the Scottish Psalter. I have little desire to print such a catalogue, astonishing as its length and seriousness would appear to many.

Let it suffice, therefore, for me to give but two examples in order to show the necessity for our publishing this new work, THE PSALMS OF THE OLD TESTAMENT.

Firstly, the rendering of the divine names — God, the LORD, The LORD God, and so on — so vital in their significance (cf. Matthew 22:41-46), is totally unreliable in the Scottish Psalter. The divine name has been arbitrarily altered no less than 288 times; added to, so as to make the name quite different, on as many as 122 occasions; and actually omitted altogether some 50 times over. This adds up to a staggering sum of 460 grave errors.

Why have they dared to do this? For no other cause than to make their task of rhyming easier.

However, none of this occurs in our translation, THE PSALMS OF THE OLD TESTAMENT. The rendering of the divine name and names can be relied upon to record just what appears in the Bible itself, so as to give that name its full value on each occasion.

The second and last example I give to demonstrate the necessity for the present work is to be found in the 119th Psalm. Central to the understanding of this psalm is the ability to distinguish between the seven words around which the fabric of the whole is woven, namely: statutes, judgments, law, commandments, precepts, word(s) and testimonies.

I say, the psalm centres upon the distinction between these seven different forms of divine expression, and the separate experience each one causes in the heart of the psalmist when taught of God. Therefore to translate each of these words correctly in the psalter is essential. Otherwise the fabric of the whole falls to pieces. But here the Scottish Psalter misleads us completely. Not only are the seven essential words frequently altered, but they are altered in such a manner as to mix and confound them together with each other. Thus, for example, as early as the second verse, the word 'testimonies' becomes 'statutes'. Again, in verse six, 'commandments' becomes 'precepts'. And so on, and on, eventually to make a total of 49 alterations, 1 addition and 5 omissions. And not in some minor or optional matter; for these are errors which confound together the very divine forms of communication without which the psalm would not have been written at all!

And why have they done such a thing, to tamper so with holy writ? Why? To make the task of rhyming easier, rather than continue the immensely difficult labour of fitting the rhyme around the correct word.

Now, to mention from the Scottish Psalter the 460 instances of altering or omitting the divine name, or to refer to the 55 cases of changing the essential wording in Psalm 119, is to cite but two of the many reasons for the writing and publishing of this entirely new and original work. I repeat, I have no desire to list others.

My desire is positive and constructive: that is, to present the psalms in the purest scriptural form possible, so that according to the Spirit and the word of God the singer may 'sing psalms unto him' in the knowledge that what is sung agrees with the psalm in the original in all that is truly essential. By this means, with joyful heart, thankful lips and instructed judgment, we shall be able to fulfil the good word of God,

> 'Teaching and admonishing one another
> in psalms and hymns and spiritual songs,
> singing with grace in your hearts
> to the Lord.'

JOHN METCALFE

THE PSALMS

PSALM 1

Jackson

1 BLESS'D is the man that walketh not
    in godless' counsel ill,
nor stands in sinners' way, nor sits
    the scornful's seat to fill.
2 But in the law that's of the LORD
    he findeth his delight;
and in his law he meditates,
    delighting day and night.

3 He'll like a tree that's planted be,
    the streams of water by,
that fruit in season bears; whose leaf
    shall wither not nor die;
Whate'er he do'th shall prosper well:
4   the godless are not so,
but like are to the chaff, which far
    the wind away doth blow.

5 The godless therefore shall not stand
    when in the judgment tried,
nor sinners in the company
    of righteous men abide.
6 Because the LORD the way doth know
    of those that righteous be:
whereas the way of godless men
    shall perish utterly.

1

PSALM 2

Petersham

1 WHY do the heathen nations rage,
  and forth their fury bring?
and wherefore do the people all
  imagine a vain thing?
2 The kings that are upon the earth
  themselves set in array;
and counsel do the rulers take;
  together gather they:

Against the LORD they speak, against
  his own anointed, thus:
3 Let us asunder break their bands
  and cast their cords from us.
4 He that doth in the heavens sit
  shall laugh at them aloud,
and wholly in derision shall
  the Lord have all the proud.

5 Then in his wrath he'll speak to them,
  and in displeasure sore
he shall afflict and trouble them,
  and vex them more and more.
6 Yet have I set my king on high
  for ever to abide;
on Zion mine own holy hill
  he shall be magnified.

7 I will declare the sure decree:
  the LORD hath said to me,
Thou art my Son; behold, this day
  have I begotten thee.
8 Ask of me, and as heritage
  the heathen give shall I:

thou shalt possess the utmost parts
    that in the earth do lie.

9 Thou'lt break them with a rod of iron;
    thou shalt them dash withal
like to a potter's vessel, dashed
    in pieces very small.
10 Be wise now therefore, O ye kings:
    instructed also be,
11 ye judges of the earth: with fear
    now serve the LORD do ye;

See that with trembling ye rejoice.
12   And do ye kiss the Son,
lest in his anger from the way
    ye perish every one,
When but a little kindled is
    his indignation just.
O blessed be that people all
    in him that put their trust.

PSALM 3

A Psalm of David,
when he fled from Absalom his son.

Belmont

1 O LORD, how much are they increased
    that trouble cause to me!
they that do up against me rise
    in number many be.
2 They many are which of my soul
    together do declare,
and say, No help in any wise
    for him in God is there.

3 But thou, O LORD, a shield thou art
  to compass me around;
 my glory, and the lifter up
  thou of mine head art found.
4 I with my voice cried to the LORD,
  and from his holy hill
5 he heard me: I laid down, slept, waked;
  the LORD sustained me still.

6 Of people I'll not be afraid,
  though thousands ten I see,
 that have against me set themselves,
  and round about me be.
7 Rise, LORD; me save, my God: for thou
  didst on the cheek-bone stout
 smite all my foes; the teeth didst thou
  of godless men break out.

8 Salvation doth unto the LORD
  most surely appertain;
 upon thy people every one
  thy blessing doth remain.

PSALM 4

To the chief Musician on Neginoth,
A Psalm of David.

Abbey

1 ME hear, God of my righteousness,
  what time I call on thee:
 thou'st me enlarged when in distress;
  have mercy, hear my plea.
2 How long will ye, O sons of men,
  to shame my glory turn?
 how long will ye love vanity,
  and after leasing yearn?

4

3 Know that the godly for himself
    the LORD apart hath set:
 the LORD when unto him I call
    to hear will not forget.

4 O stand in awe, and sin ye not:
    with your own heart do ye
 commune at rest upon your bed,
    and silent also be.

5 The sacrifices offer ye
    of righteousness most just,
 and wholly in the LORD do ye
    repose and put your trust.

6 O who will show us any good?
    there many be that say.
 The brightness of thy countenance,
    LORD, lift on us alway.

7 Thou hast put gladness in my heart,
    and joy thou hast made mine,
 more than the time that to increase
    was made their corn and wine.

8 I will both lay me down in peace,
    and restful sleep will take:
 because thou only me to dwell
    in safety, LORD, dost make.

PSALM 5
To the chief Musician upon Nehiloth,
A Psalm of David.

S. Fulbert

1 GIVE ear unto my words, O LORD,
    my meditation weigh.
2 Hear my voice cry, my King, my God,
    for I to thee will pray.

5

3 My voice thou'lt in the morning hear,
   O LORD; my prayer will I
 unto thee in the morning send,
   and will look up on high.

4 For thou art not a God that doth
   in wickedness delight;
 and neither yet shall evil find
   a dwelling in thy sight.
5 Before thine eyes there shall not stand
   those men that foolish be:
 thou hatred bearest unto all
   that work iniquity.

6 For them that leasing speak thou shalt
   slay with destruction sore:
 the bloody and deceitful man
   the LORD will e'er abhor.
7 But in thy mercy's multitude
   I'll to thy house come near:
 toward thy holy temple I
   will worship in thy fear.

8 LORD, lead me in thy righteousness,
   for my foes multiply;
 do thou before my countenance
   thy way make straight to lie.
9 For verily within their mouth
   there is no faithfulness;
 the inward part of each of them
   is very wickedness;

 Their throat's an open sepulchre;
   their tongue doth flatter all.
10 Destroy thou them, O God; let them
   by their own counsels fall.

In their transgressions' multitude
    cast out now let them be;
11 'gainst thee rebelled they: but let all
    rejoice that trust in thee;

Since thou defend'st them, let for joy
    them ever lift the voice;
let them that also love thy name
    with joy in thee rejoice.
12 For to the righteous, LORD, thou shalt
    thy blessing make abound;
with favour thou, as with a shield,
    wilt compass him around.

PSALM 6

To the chief Musician on Neginoth upon Sheminith,
A Psalm of David.

S. Agnes

1 O LORD, in this thine anger great
    do thou rebuke me not,
and neither do thou chasten me
    in thy displeasure hot.
2 Upon me mercy have, O LORD;
    for I am weak and poor:
heal me, O LORD; my bones are vexed.
3   My soul is vexed and sore:

4 But thou, O LORD, how long? Return,
    O LORD, haste do thou make
to free my soul: oh, save thou me
    for thine own mercies' sake.
5 Because of thee in death there shall
    no more remembrance be:
of those that in the grave do lie,
    who shall give thanks to thee?

6 I weary with my groaning am;
    all night, beset by fears,
I make my bed to swim; my couch
    I water with my tears.
7 Mine eye because of constant grief
    consumed and wasted is;
it waxeth old because of all
    that are mine enemies.

8 Depart, and get ye hence, all that
    do work iniquity;
because the LORD hath heard my voice
    that weepeth grievously.
9 The LORD assuredly hath heard
    my supplication's cry;
yea, know I that the LORD my prayer
    receive will from on high.

10 Let all be shamed and sorely vexed
    that en'mies are to me:
yea, let them all turn back again
    and shamed be suddenly.

PSALM 7

Shiggaion of David, which he sang unto the
LORD, concerning the words of Cush the
Benjamite.

Gloucester

1 O LORD my God, with confidence
    I put my trust in thee:
from all them that me persecute
    save and deliver me:
2 Lest like a lion he tear my soul,
    and it in pieces rend,

whilst unto me there is not one
    that can deliv'rance send.

3 O LORD my God, if I've done this,
    and guilty I have been;
or if the least iniquity
    should in my hands be seen;

4 If evil I've rewarded him
    that was at peace with me;
(yea, I have him delivered that
    my foe is causelessly:)

5 Then let the foe me persecute
    and take my soul away;
let him my life tread down on earth,
    in dust mine honour lay.

6 LORD, rise in anger, lift thyself:
    mine en'mies raging be;
O to the judgment that thou hast
    commanded, wake for me.

7 The people's congregation so
    shall compass thee around:
return thou therefore for their sakes,
    on high of them be found.

8 The LORD he shall the people judge:
    do thou, O LORD, judge me
according to my righteousness,
    and mine integrity.

9 The wicked's wickedness let end;
    the just let stablished be:
for hearts and reins the righteous God
    doth try with equity.

10 Of God's my shield, which saveth those
    upright in heart alway.

11 God doth the righteous judge; God's wroth
    with wicked men each day.

12 If he turn not, then he his sword
    assuredly will whet;
now hath he strung and bent his bow,
    it ready is and set.

13 And also instruments of death
    prepared for him hath he;
against the persecutors all
    ordained his arrows be.

14 Behold, to bear iniquity
    he hath in travail wrought;
he likewise mischief hath conceived,
    and falsehood forth hath brought.

15 He made a pit, and digged the same,
    and there a trap he laid:
but he is fallen in the ditch
    which he for others made.

16 His mischief shall return again
    and on his own head fall;
his violent dealing shall come down
    on his own pate withal.

17 According to his righteousness,
    so praise the LORD will I,
and praise sing to the name of him
    that is the LORD most high.

PSALM 8

To the chief Musician upon Gittith,
A Psalm of David.

Glasgow

1 O LORD our Lord, how excellent
    in all the earth's thy name!

thy glory's raised above the heavens,
    for there thou'st set the same.
2 Thou strength from babes' and sucklings'
    didst for thy foes ordain,   (mouth
that thou might'st the avenger still,
    the enemy restrain.

3 What time consider I thy heavens,
    and do therein behold
thy fingers' work, the moon and stars,
    ordained by thee of old;
4 Oh, what is man, that mindful thou
    of him should'st ever be?
the son of man, oh, who is this
    thus visited by thee?

5 For thou a little lower hast
    him than the angels made;
of glory and of honour thou
    a crown hast on him laid.
6 Dominion thou'st him made to have
    o'er all thy hands have wrought;
and underneath his feet thou hast
    all things created brought:

7 All sheep and oxen, yea, the beasts
    that in the field are found;
8 fowl of the air, and in the sea
    the fish that do abound;
And in the paths beneath the seas,
    what passeth through the same.
9 O Lord our Lord, how excellent
    in all the earth's thy name!

PSALM 9

To the chief Musician upon Muth-labben,
A Psalm of David.

S. Frances

1 WITH my whole heart and strength, O
I will give praise to thee; (LORD,
and I will show forth all thy works
that great and marv'llous be.

2 With gladness and with thankfulness
rejoice in thee will I:
moreover praise unto thy name
I'll sing, O thou most High.

3 When back mine enemies are turned
and overthrown by thee,
then at thy presence they shall fall,
and they destroyed shall be.

4 Because thou both my right and cause
maintained hast in thy sight;
for that thou in the throne didst sit
most surely judging right.

5 Thou hast rebuked the heathen all,
the wicked thou'st destroyed;
thou'st evermore put out their name,
and wholly made it void.

6 Thou en'my, to perpetual end
destructions all are come:
destroy'dst thou cities; perished is
their memory become.

7 But nonetheless the LORD himself
endureth evermore:
for judgment he hath set his throne,
prepared it is and sure.

8　He'll judge the world in righteousness,
　　　　and minister he shall
　　the judgment just in uprightness
　　　　unto the people all.

9　The LORD a refuge also will
　　　　for the oppressed appear;
　　behold, he will a refuge be
　　　　when troublous times are near.

10　And they that know thy name in thee
　　　　their trust will safely place,
　　for thou hast not forsaken them,
　　　　O LORD, that seek thy face.

11　O sing ye praises to the LORD,
　　　　which doth in Zion dwell:
　　among the people every one
　　　　his doings do ye tell.

12　When inquisition he for blood
　　　　doth make, them mind doth he:
　　nor doth he once forget the cry
　　　　of those that humble be.

13　Have mercy, LORD; my trouble weigh
　　　　which of my haters I
　　do suffer still, thou from death's gates
　　　　that lift'st me up on high:

14　That I may show forth all thy praise
　　　　within the gates that be
　　of Zion's daughter: I'll rejoice
　　　　in thy salvation free.

15　Behold, the heathen are sunk down
　　　　into the pit they made;
　　their own foot's taken in the net
　　　　which they in secret laid.

16 The LORD is by the judgment known
    he executes of right:
the wicked snared is in the work
    in which his hands delight.

17 So shall the wicked into hell
    be turned assuredly;
the nations all that God forget
    turned to the same shall be.
18 For those that needy are shall not
    forgotten be alway:
the expectation of the poor
    shall perish not for aye.

19 Arise, O LORD; and let not man
    prevail against thine own:
yea, let the heathen in thy sight
    be judged and overthrown.
20 Do thou them put in fear, O LORD,
    and them thy judgments show,
so that themselves to be but men
    the nations all may know.

PSALM 10

Tallis

1 WHY standest thou far off, O LORD,
    at distance from us still?
and wherefore dost thou hide thyself
    in times of trouble ill?
2 The wicked in his haughty pride
    doth persecute the poor:
them take in those devices which
    they have imagined sure.

3 The wicked in his heart's desire
   of boasting findeth cause,
and he doth bless the covetous,
   he whom the Lord abhors.
4 The wicked, through his pride of face,
   upon God will not call;
in all the musings of his thoughts
   God is not found at all.

5 For always grievous are his ways;
   and high out of his sight
thy judgments are: at all his foes
   he puffeth with despite.
6 And he hath said within his heart,
   I shall not shaken be:
throughout my days I never shall
   be in adversity.

7 For cursing and deceit and fraud
   do in his mouth abound:
beneath his tongue mischievousness
   and vanity are found.
8 In lurking places he doth sit
   the villages within:
in secret places murders he
   those innocent of sin:

For privily his eyes are set
   against the poorest men;
9 in secret lies he waiting as
   a lion in his den:
He lies in wait the poor to catch:
   and catch the poor doth he,
when he into his net him draws,
   therein ensnared to be.

10 He croucheth, and humility
    he feigns before them all,
that those bowed down with poverty
    may by his strong ones fall.

11 For he within his heart hath said,
    God hath forgotten quite:
he hides his face; he ne'er will see:
    he will not it requite.

12 O Lord, do thou arise: O God,
    lift up thine hand on high:
forget not those that humble are,
    nor turn away their cry.

13 O wherefore doth the wicked rage
    and God contemn with ire?
for he hath said within his heart,
    Thou wilt it not require.

14 Thou hast it seen; for mischief thou
    beholdest, yea, and spite,
that so in vengeance with thy hand
    thou mayest it requite.
The poor confesseth, and he doth
    commit himself to thee;
for thou the helper art of those
    that without father be.

15 The arm break of the wicked man
    that evil deeds hath done:
and seek thou out his wickedness
    until thou findest none.

16 The Lord is King by that decree
    which evermore shall stand:
the heathen peoples every one
    are perished from his land.

17 O LORD, thou the desire hast heard
    of those that humble be:
thou wilt prepare their heart, thou'lt cause
    thine ear to hear their plea:
18 To judge the fatherless, and those
    that are oppressed and poor,
that henceforth man that's of the earth
    may them oppress no more.

PSALM 11

To the chief Musician, A Psalm of David.

Abney

1 IN the LORD do put my trust:
    how can it be that ye
say to my soul, E'en as a bird
    unto your mountain flee?
2 For, lo, the wicked bend their bow,
    their shaft they ready make
upon the string, that privily
    they careful aim may take:

That after the upright in heart
    their arrows may pursue.
3 If the foundations be destroyed,
    what can the righteous do?
4 The LORD is in his holy place,
    the LORD's throne is in heav'n:
his eyes behold, his eyelids try,
    the children born of men.

5 The LORD doth try the righteous well:
    but those that wicked be,
and him that loveth violence,
    his soul hates veh'mently.

6 He on the wicked snares shall rain,
    and fire and brimstone pour:
a tempest horrible shall be
    their cup and portion sure.

7 Because the LORD that righteous is
    loves righteousness to see;
his countenance beholdeth still
    all those that upright be.

PSALM 12

To the chief Musician upon Sheminith,
A Psalm of David.

Wigtown

1 HELP, LORD; because the godly man
    out of the land doth cease;
because the faithful from men's sons
    continually decrease.
2 Each one doth words of vanity
    unto his neighbour say:
speak forth with lips of flattery
    and double heart do they.

3 The LORD in vengeance shall cut off
    all lips of flattery;
the tongue that of proud things doth speak
    requite withal shall he:
4 Those that have said, We with our tongue
    will certainly prevail;
our lips we own: who's lord o'er us?
    our strength shall us avail.

5 For the oppression of the poor,
    and for the needy's sighs,
thus saith the LORD, Behold, that I
    will even now arise;

And him in perfect safety set
   assuredly I will
from him that puffeth in his wrath
   and fury at him still.

6 The LORD's words all are words most pure,
   like unto silver tried
in earthen furnace, seven times
   refined and purified.

7 Thou shalt them safely keep, O LORD,
   and to thyself reserve;
thou from this generation shalt
   for ever them preserve.

8 The wicked walk on every side,
   what time the faithful fail;
the vilest men exalted are,
   when godless men prevail.

PSALM 13

To the chief Musician, A Psalm of David.

Kedron

1 HOW long wilt thou forget me, LORD?
   is it for evermore?
how long wilt thou conceal thy face,
   and far from me withdraw?

2 How long take counsel in my soul,
   heart-sick each day shall I?
how long shall over me my foe
   exalted be on high?

3 Consider thou, O LORD my God,
   and hear the prayer I make:
enlighten thou mine eyes, lest I
   the sleep of death should take;

4 Lest, I against him have prevailed,
     mine enemy should say;
   and those that trouble me rejoice
     when I am moved away.

5 But in thy mercy manifold
     my trust reposed have I;
   of joy in thy salvation great
     my heart shall testify.
6 And I will sing unto the LORD,
     for heretofore with me,
   in pity and in mercy great,
     dealt bountif'lly hath he.

PSALM 14

To the chief Musician, A Psalm of David.

Dundee

1 THE fool hath spoken in his heart,
       There is no God, saith he.
   They are corrupt, the works they've done
     abominations be;
   And there is none that doeth good.
2   The LORD from heaven viewed
   and on men's children looked to see
     if any understood:

   Was there but one that sought for God?
3   They all aside are gone;
   they all together filthy are,
     none do'th good, no, not one.
4 Are workers of iniquity
     all void of knowledge quite?
   who eat my people up as bread
     consuming them outright:

20

And on the LORD they do not call.
5   There fear upon them fell:
for of the righteous God doth in
    the generation dwell.
6 Ye've shamed the counsel of the poor;
    the LORD's his refuge near.
7 Oh that salvation out of Zion
    to Isr'el would appear!

When back the LORD his people brings
    from sore captivity,
then Jacob shall rejoice at last,
    and Isr'el glad shall be.

PSALM 15

A Psalm of David

Gräfenberg

1 WITHIN thy tabernacle, LORD,
        who shall abide with thee?
and in thy holy hill on high
    who shall a dweller be?
2 The man that walketh uprightly,
    and worketh righteousness,
and who the truth within his heart
    doth speak with faithfulness.

3 He with his tongue that backbites not,
    nor evil do'th to shame
his neighbour; nor reproach takes up
    against his neighbour's name.
4 In whose eyes is one vile contemned;
    but them that fear the LORD
he honoureth: sworn to his hurt,
    he changeth not his word.

5 His money he to usury
   puts not, nor bribe takes he
against the guiltless: who do'th this
   unmoved shall ever be.

Psalm 16

Michtam of David

Kilsyth

1 BECAUSE in thee I put my trust,
   preserve thou me, O God.
2 My soul, thou to the LORD hast said,
   Thou only art my Lord:
My goodness not to thee extends;
3   but unto the upright,
the saints on earth, the excellent,
   in whom's all my delight.

4 They to another god that haste
   increase their sorrows shall:
I their drink-offerings of blood
   will offer not at all;
Nor take their names up in my lips:
5   the LORD's the portion sure
of mine inheritance and cup:
   my lot thou mak'st secure.

6 The lines that fallen are to me
   in pleasant places lie;
yea, such a goodly heritage
   received from thee have I.
7 I will the LORD bless, who to me
   hath given counsel right:
my reins do also me instruct
   in seasons of the night.

8 The LORD I purposed have to set
    before me constantly:
because he is at my right hand
    I never moved shall be.

9 And even for this cause my heart
    of gladness is possessed;
my glory doth rejoice: my flesh
    in hope shall also rest.

10 For thou'lt not leave my soul in hell,
    and neither shall it be
that thou corruption suffer wilt
    thine Holy One to see.

11 Thou wilt me show the path of life:
    of joy is fulness found
within thy presence; pleasures aye
    at thy right hand abound.

PSALM 17

A Prayer of David

S. Peter

1 INCLINE and hear the right, O LORD,
    unto my cry attend,
give ear unto my prayer, which I
    from unfeigned lips do send.

2 Swift from thy presence let there come
    my sentence forth to me;
the things that equal are now let
    thine eyes behold and see.

3 Thou'st proved my heart; thou'st visited
    by night, me to assess;
thou'lt nothing find; I'm purposed that
    my mouth shall not transgress.

4 Concerning works that to themselves
    men's sons do multiply,
  myself from the destroyer's paths
    by thy lips' word kept I.

5 Hold up my goings in thy paths,
    that my steps may not slide.
6 Because thou wilt me hear, O God,
    I unto thee have cried:
  Incline thou unto me thine ear,
    and hearken to my speech.
7 Thy loving-kindness marvellous
    me show, I thee beseech,

  O thou that sav'st by thy right hand
    them which do trust in thee
  from those which in their violence
    against them risen be.
8 Like as the apple of the eye
    with thee let me abide;
  beneath the shadow of thy wings
    do thou me safely hide,

9 From wicked men that me oppress,
    and seek to blot me out,
  and from my deadly enemies
    that compass me about.
10 They are enclosed in their own fat:
    their mouth and speech is proud.
11 They have us compassed in our steps:
    eyes set, to earth down bowed;

12 Like as a lion that of prey
    is greedy to be fed,
  and as a lion young that lurks
    in secret places dread.

13 Arise, do thou him disappoint,
    and cast him down, O Lord:
deliver thou my soul from him,
    the wicked, thine own sword:

14 From men which are thy hand, O Lord,
    from worldly men and ill,
which have their portion in this life,
    whose belly thou dost fill;
As with thy treasure hid, they're full
    of children they conceive;
and of their substance they the rest
    unto their babes do leave.

15 But as for me, in righteousness
    thy face I'll surely see:
and with thy likeness, when I wake,
    I satisfied shall be.

Psalm 18

To the chief Musician, A Psalm of David, the
servant of the Lord, who spake unto the Lord
the words of this song in the day that the Lord
delivered him from the hand of all his enemies,
and from the hand of Saul: And he said,

Old 18th

1 THEE will I love, O Lord, my strength.
2   The Lord my rock is he,
my fortress, and the one that brings
    deliverance to me;
My God, my strength, in whom I trust;
    my buckler firm and sure,
the horn of my salvation strong,
    and my high tower secure.

3 Upon the LORD, who to be praised
    is worthy, I will call:
  so from mine en'mies round about
    be saved and freed I shall.
4 Death's sorrows compassed me, the floods
    of ill men made me fear.
5 Hell's sorrows compassed me, death's snares
    before me did appear.

6 I from the depths upon the LORD
    did call in my distress,
  and in my grief unto my God
    my cry I did express:
  He from his temple heard my voice,
    and hearkened to my cry;
  my prayer before him even came
    into his ears on high.

7 Then did the earth with trembling shake;
    and, moved exceedingly,
  the hills' foundations shaken were,
    because that wroth was he.
8 Out of his nostrils went a smoke,
    himself he did bestir:
  out of his mouth a fire devoured;
    coals by it kindled were.

9 He also did the heavens bow,
    and came down from on high:
  and underneath his feet, as night,
    thick darkness veiled the sky.
10 And he upon a cherub rode,
    and flew in his descent:
  yea, he did fly upon the wings
    that of the wind were sent.

11 He darkness made his secret place:
    dark waters did arise
  which round him his pavilion were,
    with thick clouds of the skies.
12 And at the burning brightness that
    before him was afire,
  the denseness of his clouds did pass,
    hailstones and coals of fire.

13 The Lord he also in the heavens
    did thunder in his ire,
  aloud the Highest gave his voice;
    hailstones and coals of fire.
14 Yea, he his arrows sent, and them
    he scattered, that they fled;
  moreover lightnings he shot out
    and them discomfited.

15 Then were the waters' channels seen,
    the world's foundations vast
  discovered were at thy rebuke,
    Lord, at thy nostrils' blast.
16 He sent forth from his place above,
    me safely take did he,
  he drew me out of places deep
    where many waters be.

17 He set me free from my strong foe,
    and them which did me hate:
  because in strength, when they arose,
    they were for me too great.
18 They me prevented in the day
    of my calamity:
  but yet the Lord became a stay
    and strong support to me.

19 Into a large and wealthy place
  he also forth me brought:
because in me he took delight
  he my deliv'rance wrought.
20 According to my righteousness,
  the LORD rewarded me;
according as my hands were clean,
  me recompensed hath he.

21 The LORD's ways I failed not to keep,
  nor from my God did fall
22 through wickedness: before me were
  his righteous judgments all;
His statutes from me I put not:
23   before him uprightly
I also walked; I kept myself
  from mine iniquity.

24 Thus hath the LORD me recompensed
  after my righteousness,
after the cleanness that my hands
  did in his sight possess.
25 Thou mercy show'st to merciful;
  to upright, thou'rt upright;
26 pure to the pure; but froward thou
  art in the froward's sight.

27 Thou'lt save afflicted people, but
28   high looks bring down: thou'lt still
my candle light: the LORD my God
  my darkness lighten will.
29 For by thee I've run through a troop,
  by my God leaped a wall.
30 As for God, perfect is his way:
  the LORD's word's tried withal:

He is a buckler to all them
    that trust in him afford.
31 Who save the LORD is God? or who
    a rock is save our God?
32 God girdeth me with strength; my way
    he perfect makes to lie,
33 my feet like hinds' feet makes, and sets
    me on my places high.

34 My hands he trains to war, mine arms
    a bow of steel to break.
35 The shield of thy salvation thou
    hast given me to take:
For thy right hand hath holden me,
    a strong support and stay;
thy gentleness hath made me great,
    encompassing my way.

36 My steps thou in thy faithfulness
    enlarged hast under me,
so that upon the way my feet
    were kept from slipping free.
37 Mine enemies I have pursued,
    and them did overtake:
I neither turned again till I
    an end of them did make.

38 I by my sword have wounded them,
    and brought them to defeat:
they cannot rise again, for they
    are fallen 'neath my feet.
39 With strength thou'st girded me to fight
    in battle 'gainst my foes:
thou hast subdued them under me
    that up against me rose.

40 Thou'st given me the necks of all
      mine enemies that be;
   that them I might destroy and slay
      that haters are to me.

41 They cried, but there was none to save,
      none answered to their call;
   they cried unto the LORD, but them
      he answered not at all.

42 Then did I beat them small as dust
      before the wind to fly:
   I cast them out just as the dirt
      that in the streets doth lie.

43 Thou hast delivered me from all
      the people's strivings vain;
   and of the heathen as the head
      thou hast me made to reign:

   A race I've known not shall me serve:
44   as soon as they have heard
   they'll me obey: submit themselves
      shall strangers to my word.

45 The strangers then shall fade away,
      and from close places fear.

46 The LORD doth live! Bless'd be my rock,
      my stronghold ever near;

   The God of my salvation great
      let high exalted be.

47 God me avengeth, and subdues
      the people under me.

48 He me delivers from the foe
      that 'gainst me multiplies:
   yea, thou dost lift me over them
      that up against me rise:

Thou'st freed me from the violent man:
49   I'll therefore thanks proclaim
to thee, LORD, 'mong the heathen, and
    sing praises to thy name.
50 Deliv'rance great he gives his king;
    and showeth mercy sure
to his anointed, David, and
    to his seed evermore.

PSALM 19

To the chief Musician, A Psalm of David.

Moravia

1 THE heav'ns God's glory do declare,
    the firmament doth teach
2 his handiwork: day unto day
    doth also utter speech;
Night unto night doth knowledge show:
3   no speech nor tongue doth sound
4 where is their voice unheard: their line
    throughout the earth is found;

And to the end of all the world
    their words run constantly.
In them a tabernacle great
    set for the sun hath he:
5 Which from his chamber coming out
    is as a bridegroom young,
and as a man to run a race
    that joyful is and strong.

6 His going forth's from heaven's end,
    his circuit to its ends:
and there is nothing to be found
    hid from the heat it sends.

7 The Lord's law's perfect, and converts
    the soul that helpless lies:
the Lord's own testimony's sure,
    the simple making wise.

8 The statutes of the Lord are right,
    and do rejoice the heart:
the Lord's commandment's pure, and doth
    light to the eyes impart.

9 Clean is the Lord's fear, and endures
    for ever in his sight:
true are the judgments of the Lord,
    and altogether right.

10 To be desired much more than gold,
    yea, much fine gold, they are:
than honey and the honeycomb
    they're also sweeter far.

11 Moreover warned thy servant is
    by these thy judgments sound:
and in the keeping of the same
    there great reward is found.

12 Who can his errors know? Me cleanse
    from secret faults, I pray:

13 thy servant from presumptuous sins
    keep also back alway;
Dominion over me let them
    not have: then shall I be
upright and innocent, and from
    the great transgression free.

14 Acceptable let my mouth's words,
    and heart's reflection, too,
be in thy sight, O Lord, my strength,
    and my redeemer true.

PSALM 20

To the chief Musician, A Psalm of David.

Kilmarnock

1 THE LORD unto thee in the day
    of trouble sore give ear;
and may the name of Jacob's God
    for thy defence appear;
2 Help from the sanctuary send,
    from Zion give thee aid;
3 remember all the offerings
    which thou to him hast made;

And thy burnt sacrifice accept,
    when thou dost on him call;
4 grant thee according to thine heart,
    fulfil thy counsel all.
5 In thy salvation we'll rejoice,
    we in our God's name will
set up our banners: and thy pleas
    all may the LORD fulfil.

6 Now know I his anointed doth
    the LORD save; he'll at length
hear from his holy heaven with
    his right hand's saving strength.
7 In chariots some put trust, and some
    in horses trust afford:
but we remember will the name
    that's of the LORD our God.

8 They are brought down and fallen lie:
    but risen are we all,
9 and upright stand: save, LORD, and let
    the king hear when we call.

PSALM 21

To the chief Musician, A Psalm of David.

Sheffield

1 THE king shall joy in this thy strength,
  O LORD, with gladsome voice;
 and in thine own salvation free,
  how greatly he'll rejoice!
2 Thou'st given him his heart's desire
  which he to thee expressed,
 and of his lips thou hast not once
  withholden the request.

3 With blessings thou dost him prevent
  of goodness manifold:
 thou settest on his head a crown
  that is of purest gold.
4 Moreover thou didst give him life,
  when this he asked of thee;
 thou gav'st him even length of days
  that evermore shall be.

5 In that salvation by thee wrought
  his glory great is made:
 for honour high and majesty
  thou hast upon him laid.
6 For him most blessed made hast thou
  for ever by thy grace:
 and thou exceeding glad withal
  hast made him with thy face.

7 Because the king's sure confidence
  doth in the LORD abide,
 and through the most High's mercy he
  shall not be moved aside.

34

8 Thine hand shall find out all that are
    thine enemies and foes:
thy right hand shall them find out that
    with hatred thee oppose.

9 Them thou'lt a fiery oven make
    when kindled is thine ire:
the LORD shall swallow them in wrath,
    devour them shall the fire.

10 Thou'lt from the earth destroy the fruit
    which forth from them doth spring,
and shalt their seed from 'mong men's sons
    unto destruction bring.

11 'Gainst thee they evil did intend:
    imagined they to form
a mischievous and ill device,
    which they cannot perform.

12 Thou'lt therefore make them turn their back,
    when thou shalt ready place
thine arrows sharp upon thy strings
    to fly against their face.

13 Be thou exalted, LORD, and raised
    above in thine own strength;
so we with thankful voice shall sing
    and praise thy pow'r at length.

PSALM 22

To the chief Musician upon Aijeleth Shahar,
A Psalm of David.

Old 22nd

1 MY God, my God, why hast thou me
    forsaken? why so far
art thou from helping me, and from
    my words that roaring are?

2 My God, I in the daytime cry,
    but am not heard by thee;
  and in the season of the night
    I cannot silent be.

3 But thou art holy, thou that dost
    in Isr'el's praises dwell.
4 Our fathers put their trust in thee,
    they trusted thee right well;
  And thou wast their deliverer.
5   They cried: deliv'rance found:
  because they put their trust in thee,
    them thou didst not confound.

6 But I a worm and no man am;
    of men I am apprized
  a sore reproach: and I of all
    the people am despised.
7 All they that see me at me mock,
    laugh me to scorn do they:
  moreover shooting out the lip,
    they shake the head, and say,

8 Upon the Lord he trusted that
    deliver him would he:
  let him deliver, since he such
    delight in him did see.
9 But thou art he that from the womb
    did at the first me take:
  when I was on my mother's breasts
    thou me to hope didst make.

10 I even from the womb was cast
    in helplessness on thee:
  thou from my mother's belly art
    my God assuredly.

11 Be not far off; for trouble's near;
 for none to help is found.
12 Bulls many compassed me: strong bulls
 of Bashan me surround.

13 They gaped upon me with their mouths,
 upon me yawn did they,
like as a lion ravening
 and roaring for his prey.
14 I like to water am poured out,
 my bones disjointed be:
my heart's like wax; amidst my bowels
 it melted is in me.

15 My strength is like a potsherd dried;
 my tongue it cleaveth fast
unto my jaws; and in the dust
 of death thou hast me cast.
16 For dogs have compassed me about:
 the wicked, that did meet
in their assembly, me enclosed:
 they pierced my hands and feet.

17 I all my bones may tell: they looked
 and stared that by me passed:
18 they 'mong them part my clothes, and lots
 upon my vesture cast.
19 But be not far, LORD: O my strength,
 make haste and help thou me.
20 My soul from sword, my darling from
 the dog's pow'r, set thou free.

21 Out of the rav'ning lion's mouth
 to save me draw thou nigh:
for from the horns of unicorns
 thou'st hearkened to my cry.

22 To those that brethren are to me
   I will declare thy name:
   amidst the congregation great
   thy praise I will proclaim.

23 Ye that the LORD do fear, him praise;
   ye seed of Jacob all,
   him glorify; all Isr'el's seed,
   do ye him fear withal.

24 For he despised not nor abhorred
   the poor man's poverty;
   nor hid from him his face, but heard
   when cry to him did he.

25 My praise shall be of thee within
   the congregation great:
   my vows I'll pay before them that
   in fear upon him wait.

26 The meek shall eat, and be well filled:
   and they their praise shall give
   unto the LORD that do him seek:
   your heart shall ever live.

27 The world's ends to the LORD shall turn
   what time remember they:
   the kindreds of the nations all
   to thee shall homage pay.

28 The kingdom is the LORD's: and he
   doth govern nations all.

29 They that be fat upon the earth
   both eat and worship shall:

   They shall each one before him bow
   that to the dust go down:
   and none of them can keep alive
   the soul that is his own.

30 There for his service shall a seed
  be unto him assured;
it for a generation shall
  be counted to the Lord.

31 They come shall, and his righteousness
  by them declared shall be
unto a people not yet born,
  that done these things hath he.

PSALM 23

A Psalm of David

Crimond

1 THE LORD's my shepherd, I'll not want.
2   In pastures green doth he
make me to lie, and he beside
  still waters leadeth me.
3 'Tis he that doth restore my soul:
  he leadeth me to take
my way in paths of righteousness,
  e'en for his own name's sake.

4 Yea, though I walk death's shadowed vale,
  yet will I fear no ill:
for thou art with me, and thy rod
  and staff me comfort still.
5 A table thou'st prepared for me
  in presence of my foes:
my head with oil thou dost anoint,
  and my cup overflows.

6 Goodness and mercy all my days
  shall surely follow me:
and in the LORD's house evermore
  my dwelling-place shall be.

PSALM 24

A Psalm of David

Petersham

1 THE earth's the LORD's, and all that doth
    within the same abound;
2 the world, and all therein: for he
    did on the seas it found;
He stablished it upon the floods,
    and settled it remains.
3 Who shall ascend into the hill
    that to the LORD pertains?

Who in his holy place shall stand?
4   The man whose hands are clean,
whose heart is pure; to vanity
    whose soul's not lifted been;
Who hath not sworn deceitfully.
5   The blessing from the LORD
he shall receive, and righteousness
    from his salvation's God.

6 This is the generation called,
    yea, this the chosen race,
of those that do him seek, that do
    O Jacob, seek thy face.
7 Lift up your heads, ye gates; lift up,
    ye doors that lasting be:
the King of glory shall come in;
    in triumph come shall he.

8 But who of glory is this King?
    The mighty LORD and strong;
the LORD it is, to whom the might
    in battle doth belong.

9   Lift up your heads, ye gates; e'en lift,
     ye doors that lasting be:
  the King of glory shall come in;
     in triumph come shall he.

10 But who of glory is this King?
     The LORD of hosts it is,
  both mighty and victorious,
     the King of glory this!   (repeat verse 1)

PSALM 25

A Psalm of David

Selma (short metre)

1 O LORD, I unto thee
    do lift my soul on high.
2 My God, let me not be ashamed,
    for trust in thee do I;
  Let not exult o'er me
    my foes that do me hate.
3 Yea, let not them be put to shame
    that do upon thee wait:

  Who without cause transgress
    let sore confounded be.
4 Show unto me thy ways, O LORD,
    and teach thy paths to me.
5 O lead me in thy truth,
    and teach thou me thy way:
  for thou art my salvation's God;
    on thee I wait all day.

6 Remember thou, O LORD,
    thy tender mercies sure,
  and all thy loving-kindnesses,
    for they of old endure.

7 Youth's sins remember not,
    nor my transgressions see:
according to thy mercy great
    do thou remember me;

    Yea, for thy goodness' sake,
    O LORD, to mind me call.
8 For good and upright is the LORD,
    and just in his ways all:
He'll therefore sinners teach
    that in the way him seek.
9 The meek in judgment he will guide:
    his way he'll teach the meek.

10 In mercy and in truth
    the LORD's paths all are sure,
to such as keep his covenant
    and testimonies pure.
11 LORD, for thine own name's sake,
    I pray, and on thee wait,
O pardon mine iniquity,
    for it is very great.

12 What man doth fear the LORD,
    and would his servant be?
him shall he in the way instruct
    that choose for him shall he.
13 His soul shall dwell at ease:
    no ill shall him befall;
moreover after him his seed
    the earth inherit shall.

14 The secret of the LORD
    with them that fear him is;
and he himself will show to them
    the cov'nant that is his.

15 Mine eyes toward the LORD
    continually are set;
for he it is that shall pluck forth
    my feet out of the net.

16 Now turn thee unto me,
    and mercy to me show;
because I am made desolate,
    and am afflicted so.

17 The troubles of my heart
    enlarged are to my grief:
from out of my distresses all,
    O bring thou me relief.

18 On mine affliction look;
    my pain wilt thou not see?
wilt thou not all my sins forgive,
    and pardon grant to me?

19 Consider thou my foes,
    which many are and great:
for it a cruel hatred is
    wherewith they do me hate.

20 O do thou keep my soul;
    do thou deliver me:
let me not be ashamed, because
    I put my trust in thee.

21 Let now integrity
    and uprightness, I pray,
preserve and keep me safe, for I
    upon thee wait all day.

22 Redeem thou Israel;
    his grief to mind recall:
redemption to him send, O God,
    out of his troubles all.

PSALM 26

A Psalm of David

S. Bernard

1 IN mine integrity I've walked:
    me judge, O LORD, and try;
I've also trusted in the LORD:
    slide therefore shall not I.

2 Examine and me prove, O LORD;
    my reins and heart apprize:

3 because thy loving-kindness I
    do keep before mine eyes:

4 I've in thy truth walked. I've not sat
    with men of vanity;
I neither will go in with those
    that vain dissemblers be.

5 The congregation hated I
    of evil-doers proud;
with wicked men myself to sit
    I have not once allowed.

6 In innocency I mine hands
    will wash, and clean be found:
and so thine altar I, O LORD,
    will surely compass round:

7 That so I with thanksgiving's voice
    may publish joyfully,
and tell abroad of all thy works
    that great and wondrous be.

8 The habitation of thy house
    I have, O LORD, loved well;
and I have also loved the place
    where doth thine honour dwell.

9 With sinners gather not my soul,
     with bloody men my life,
10 whose hands work mischief; full of bribes,
     their right hand worketh strife.

11 But as for me, I will walk on
     in mine integrity:
   redeem thou me, I pray, and still
     be merciful to me.
12 My foot is in an even place,
     and there doth stand assured:
   I in the congregations will
     most surely bless the LORD.

PSALM 27

A Psalm of David

Stroudwater

1 THE LORD's my light and saving strength;
       whom therefore shall I fear?
   my life's strength is the LORD; of whom
     shall I afraid appear?
2 When wicked men, mine enemies,
     my foes and haters all,
   upon me came to eat my flesh,
     they stumbled and did fall.

3 Against me though an host encamp,
     my heart shall fear no ill;
   though war should rise against me, yet
     be confident I will:
4 One thing I've of the LORD desired,
     that will I seek right well:
   that all days of my life I may
     within the LORD's house dwell;

That I the beauty of the LORD
    behold may and admire,
and that within his temple I
    may constantly inquire.

5 In his pavilion he'll me hide
    when grief doth me befall:
he hide me in the secret of
    his tabernacle shall;

He on a rock shall set me up.
6   And now lift up shall he
mine head above mine enemies
    that round about me be:
I in his tabernacle will
    joy's sacrifices bring;
and I will sing, yea, to the LORD
    with praises I will sing.

7 Attend, O LORD, and do thou hear,
    when with my voice I cry:
upon me also mercy have,
    and answer from on high.
8 When thou didst say, Seek ye my face,
    then unto thee reply
thus did my heart, Thy face, O LORD,
    seek earnestly will I.

9 Far from me hide not thou thy face;
    put not away from thee
thy servant in thy wrath: for thou
    hast been an help to me.
Me leave not, nor forsake at all,
    O my salvation's God.
10 When father, mother, me forsake,
    me take up will the LORD.

11 Teach unto me thy way, O LORD,
  and I the same shall heed;
because of all mine enemies
  me in a plain path lead.

12 Yield me not to mine en'mies' will:
  for 'gainst me risen be
those that bear witness false, and such
  as breathe out cruelty.

13 I fainted had, unless at length
  I had believed to see
the LORD's own goodness in the land
  of those that living be.

14 Wait on the LORD: good courage have,
  and he shall strength afford
unto thine heart; yea, do thou wait,
  I say, upon the LORD.

PSALM 28

A Psalm of David

Gloucester

1 TO thee I'll cry, O LORD my rock;
  hold not thy peace to me:
lest like them that go down the pit
  I by thy silence be.

2 Hear thou my supplications' voice,
  when unto thee I cry,
when to thy holy oracle
  I lift my hands on high.

3 Me draw not with ill men, nor those
  that work iniquity,
which to their friends speak peace, whilst they
  in heart mischievous be.

47

4 After their deeds them give, as they
        through wickedness did earn:
   after their handiwork them give;
        them their desert return.

5 Since they the LORD's works would not heed,
        nor of his hands would see
   the operation, them cast down
        and not build up shall he.

6 For ever blessed be the LORD,
        because he from on high
   hath heard my supplications' voice,
        and answered hath my cry.

7 The LORD my strength is and my shield;
        on him my heart relied,
   and I am helped: therefore my heart
        in gladness doth abide;
   And with my song I will him praise.

8   The LORD's their strength alone;
   he also is the saving strength
        of his anointed one.

9 Thy people save, and do thou bless
        thy heritage always:
   them also feed, and do thou them
        for evermore upraise.

PSALM 29

A Psalm of David

Crediton

1 O DO ye give unto the LORD,
        all ye that mighty be,
   give all the glory and the strength
        unto the LORD do ye:

48

2 Yea, to the LORD the glory due
    unto his name afford:
in beauty wrought of holiness,
    O worship ye the LORD.

3 The LORD's voice on the waters sounds:
    the God of glory this!
he thunders: for the LORD himself
    on many waters is.
4 The LORD's voice soundeth full of power,
    a mighty voice hath he;
the LORD's voice hath a kingly sound,
    'tis full of majesty.

5 The LORD's voice doth the cedars break,
    and they before it fall;
yea, for the LORD in Lebanon
    doth break the cedars tall.
6 He doth them also make to skip
    · like to a calf new-born;
both Lebanon and Sirion,
    like a young unicorn.

7 The LORD's voice doth divide in twain
    and rend the flames of fire.
8 The LORD's voice from on high doth shake
    the wilderness entire;
The LORD doth cause the wilderness
    of Kadesh all to shake.
9 The LORD's voice sounding in its strength
    the hinds to calve doth make,

And doth the forests by its power
    discover and make bare:
and in his temple every one
    his glory doth declare.

10 The LORD doth sit upon the flood,
    and over all is he;
yea, evermore the LORD as King
    doth sit in majesty.

11 The LORD unto his people strength
    most plenteously will give;
the LORD will bless his people all
    that they in peace might live.

PSALM 30

A Psalm and Song
at the dedication of the house of David

S. David

1 I'LL thee extol, O LORD, because
    thou hast uplifted me,
and o'er me hast not made my foes
    rejoice exceedingly.
2 O LORD my God, to thee I cried,
    thou'st healed and made me whole:
3 O LORD, and even from the grave
    thou hast brought up my soul.

Thou hast me safely kept alive,
    that I should not go down
4 into the pit. Sing to the LORD,
    O ye his saints each one.
And give him thanks when ye do call
    his holiness to mind.
5 For but a moment lasts his wrath:
    life's in his favour kind.

To weep may for a night endure:
    but morn doth joy recall.
6 In my prosperity I said,
    I'll not be moved at all.

7 My mountain strong to stand, O Lord,
    thou'st by thy favour made:
but thou didst hide thy face, and I
    was troubled and dismayed.

8 I lifted up my voice and cried
    to thee, O Lord, alone;
and I unto the Lord did make
    my supplication known.

9 What profit's in my blood, when down
    into the pit I go?
shall thee the dust praise? or thy truth
    shall it declare and show?

10 Hear, Lord, and on me mercy have:
    O Lord, my helper be.
11 Thou into joyful dancing hast
    my mourning turned for me:
My sackcloth thou'st from me put off,
    and hast it cast aside:
with gladness thou hast girded me,
    and made my joy abide;

12 Unto the end that sing to thee
    my glory may in praise,
and not be silent. Lord my God,
    I'll give thee thanks always.

PSALM 31

To the chief Musician, A Psalm of David.

Belmont

1 IN thee, O Lord, I put my trust;
    shamed let me never be:
give ear, and in thy righteousness
    do thou deliver me.

51

2 And unto me bow down thine ear;
    with speed deliv'rance send:
  be my strong rock, and for an house
    to save and me defend.

3 For thou my rock and fortress art,
    in which I safely hide;
  for thy name's sake me therefore lead,
    and me with counsel guide.

4 Because thou art become my strength,
    me pull out of the net,
  which for me in their enmity
    they privily have set.

5 For I into thine hand commit
    my spirit: thou art he,
  O thou LORD God of truth, that hast
    redemption sent to me.

6 I truly have each one of them
    detested and abhorred
  that lying vanities regard:
    but I trust in the LORD.

7 I in thy mercy will be glad,
    and joy exceedingly:
  because thou hast considered well
    my sore calamity;
  For thou hast known my soul when through
    adversities brought low,

8 and hast not shut me up into
    the strong hand of the foe:

  Thou in a large room stablished hast
    and made my feet stand fast.

9 Have mercy on me, LORD, for I
    in trouble sore am cast:

Mine eye with grief consumed is, yea,
 my soul and belly waste:
10 my life with grief is quite spent up,
 my years with sighing haste:

My strength fails through iniquity;
 my bones consume thereby.
11 Among each of mine enemies
 a sore reproach was I,
But more especially among
 my neighbours that were near;
and unto mine acquaintance close
 became I as a fear:

They also that me saw without
 far from my presence fled.
12 I am forgotten, out of mind,
 like to a man long dead:
I like a broken vessel am.
13 For whispered in mine ear
the slander I of many heard:
 on every side was fear:

While 'gainst me counsel privily
 together take did they,
a cruel device they did devise
 to take my life away.
14 But I, O LORD, in thee did trust:
 I said, Thou art my God.
15 My times are ever in thy hand:
 thine help to me afford;

And from the hand of all my foes
 do thou deliver me;
and from them that me persecute
 me also set thou free.

16 And so thy face to shine anew
    upon thy servant make:
moreover hear and do me save,
    e'en for thy mercies' sake.

17 Let me not be ashamed, O LORD;
    for I have called on thee:
the wicked shame, and in the grave
    made silent let them be.

18 Let silent be the lying lips,
    which grievous things and ill
speak proudly and contemptuously
    against the righteous still.

19 How great's thy goodness thou'st for them
    that fear thee laid in store;
which thou'st for them wrought that thee trust
    the sons of men before!

20 Thou shalt them in the secret place
    of thine own presence hide;
thou shalt in safety them preserve,
    and keep them from man's pride:

In a pavilion thou'lt sustain
    and keep them secretly
from tongues against them lifted up
    in strife and enmity.

21 O blessed be the LORD, for he
    hath to me magnified
his kindness marvellous within
    a city fortified.

22 For I had spoken in my haste,
    and was in speech unwise;
because I said, I am cut off,
    e'en from before thine eyes:

But nonetheless thou heard'st my voice
  in supplication made,
when I had cried aloud in fear,
  and unto thee had prayed.

23 O love the LORD, all ye his saints:
    the faithful doth the LORD
preserve, and the proud doer he
    doth plenteously reward.
24 Be of good courage, and your heart
    with strength he shall supply,
all ye with hope and confidence
    that on the LORD rely.

PSALM 32

A Psalm of David, Maschil.

Westminster

1 HE happy is and bless'd whose guilt
      forgiven is and past,
he whose transgression pardoned is,
    whose sin thou covered hast.
2 Yea, happy is the man and blessed
    to whom iniquity
the LORD imputeth not; from guile
    whose spirit is made free.

3 When I kept silence, then my bones
    waxed old through roaring strong
that I did make, for in my grief
    I roared the whole day long.
4 For day and night upon me pressed
    thine hand did heavy lie;
so that e'en into summer's drought
    my moisture's turned thereby.

5 I thereupon my grievous sin
    acknowledged unto thee,
and from thee have I hidden none
    of mine iniquity.
All my transgressions to the LORD
    I will confess, said I;
and from my sin's iniquity
    thou didst me justify.

6 For this shall every godly one
    pray earnestly to thee,
and make entreaty in a time
    when found thou mayest be:
For when the floods of waters great
    be risen up on high,
then surely they shall not be heard,
    nor unto him draw nigh.

7 Thou art my hiding-place; thou shalt
    from trouble keep me free;
thou with songs of deliverance
    about shalt compass me.
8 Thee in the way which thou shalt go
    instruct and teach will I:
I will thee lead assuredly,
    and guide thee with mine eye.

9 Be ye not as the horse or mule,
    which void of knowledge be:
with bit and bridle their mouth's held,
    lest they come near to thee.
10 For many ills and sorrows are
    the wicked's own reward:
but mercy shall him compass round
    that trusteth in the LORD.

11 Now therefore in the LORD be glad,
    rejoice with all your might,
ye righteous: shout for joy, all ye
    in heart that are upright.

PSALM 33

Forest Green

1 O YE that righteous are, rejoice
    and in the LORD delight:
for praise is comely for all those
    that are in truth upright.
2 With harp the LORD praise, and to him
    with psaltery give voice:
upon a ten-stringed instrument
    with songs do ye rejoice.

3 A new song sing ye unto him;
    a loud noise play with skill.
4 For right's the LORD's word; all his works
    in truth he doth fulfil.
5 To righteousness and judgment he
    a steadfast love maintains:
the earth is of the goodness full
    that to the LORD pertains.

6 The heavens by the LORD were made
    when he the word but spake;
and all their host by his mouth's breath
    their form at first did take.
7 He gathers waters of the sea
    together as an heap:
he layeth up the depth as in
    storehouses of the deep.

8 Oh, let the whole earth fear the LORD,
   and tremble him before;
and let the world's inhabitants
   of him all stand in awe.
9 For he but spake, and it was done,
   by his own word secured:
he did command, and it stood fast,
   'twas by his speech assured.

10 The LORD the counsel brings to nought
   which godless heathen take;
the people's bold devices he
   of none effect doth make.
11 The counsel of the LORD doth stand
   for ever past recall,
and of his heart the thoughts abide
   to generations all.

12 That nation blessed is whose God
   the LORD is; and alone
the people he as heritage
   hath chosen for his own.
13 The LORD from heaven looketh down,
   and there beholdeth he
upon the face of all the earth
   the sons of men that be.

14 For from the place where he resides,
   his habitation high,
he all the earth's inhabitants
   before him doth espy.
15 He fashioneth their hearts as one,
   alike he doth them frame;
and all their works he ponders well,
   considering the same.

16 By an host great in multitude
   no king shall safety see:
   and by much strength a mighty man
   shall not delivered be.

17 An horse for safety doth appear
   a vain and helpless thing:
   by his great strength he unto none
   deliverance can bring.

18 Behold, on them that do him fear
   the LORD's eye doth abide,
   on them that in his mercy great
   their hope and trust confide;

19 To save their soul from death: to keep
   their life from famine free.

20 O for the LORD our soul doth wait:
   our help and shield is he.

21 For in him shall our heart rejoice
   and shall his praise proclaim,
   because with joy we have our trust
   placed in his holy name.

22 Let now thy mercy plentiful,
   O LORD, upon us be,
   according as with confidence
   we put our hope in thee.

PSALM 34

A Psalm of David, when he changed his
behaviour before Abimelech; who drove him
away, and he departed.   S. James

1 I WILL at all times bless the LORD:
       his praise continually
   throughout my days with thankfulness
   found in my mouth shall be.

2 My soul shall also in the LORD
    her boast with meekness make:
the humble all shall hear thereof,
    and glad be for my sake.

3 O magnify the LORD with me
    and him with praise acclaim;
let us together lift the voice
    and so exalt his name.

4 I sought the LORD, he did me hear
    and from distress set free:
yea, from my fears and troubles all
    he did deliver me.

5 They also unto him did look,
    and lightened they became:
and of their countenances all
    not one was put to shame.

6 This poor man cried, the LORD did hear,
    and him an answer gave:
from out of all his troubles great
    he surely did him save.

7 The angel of the LORD encamps
    about them that him fear,
and doth for their deliverance
    in time of need appear.

8 O do ye taste and see that good
    at all times is the LORD:
he to the man that trusts in him
    his blessing doth afford.

9 O do ye fear the LORD, his saints:
    no want shall them betide,
nor shall they know the smallest lack,
    that in his fear abide.

10 The lions young do lack and pine,
    and suffer hunger so:
but they that seek the LORD want not,
    nor any good forgo.

11 O come, ye children, unto me,
    and hearken to my speech:
for in my doctrine unto you
    I will the LORD's fear teach.

12 Who life desires, loves many days,
    that good would see the while?

13 Thy tongue from evil do thou keep,
    thy lips from speaking guile.

14 Depart from evil, and do good;
    seek peace, and it pursue.

15 The LORD's eyes mark the just, his ears
    attend their crying too.

16 The LORD's face is against them set
    that evil-doers be,
remembrance of them from the earth
    to cut off utterly.

17 The righteous cry, the LORD doth hear,
    attending to their call;
and straightway he delivers them
    out of their troubles all.

18 The LORD is nigh unto them that
    are of a broken heart;
to those of contrite spirit he
    salvation doth impart.

19 Full many the afflictions are
    which to the righteous be:
but him the LORD delivereth,
    and from them all doth free.

20 He keepeth all his bones unharmed,
  he all of them doth tell:
not one of them is broken, yea,
  he keepeth them right well.

21 But evil shall the wicked slay.
  They that the righteous hate
shall be cut off, they'll not abide:
  they shall be desolate.
22 The LORD redeems the soul of them
  that do upon him wait;
and none of them that trust in him
  shall be made desolate.

PSALM 35

A Psalm of David

S. Anne

1 RISE up and plead my cause, O LORD,
  with them that strive with me:
against them also do thou fight
  that 'gainst me fighters be.
2 Of shield and buckler take thou hold,
  and for mine help appear,
yea, do thou for mine help stand up,
3   draw also out the spear;

Against them do thou stop the way
  that persecute me sore:
and do thou say unto my soul,
  I'm thy salvation sure.
4 Let them confounded be and shamed
  that for my soul have sought:
who scheme my hurt let be turned back
  and to confusion brought.

5 Let them be even as the chaff
　　before the wind that's blown:
　them let the angel of the LORD
　　chase till they're overthrown.
6 Let closed about with darkness deep
　　and slipp'ry be their way:
　and let the angel of the LORD
　　them persecute alway.

7 For without cause they've hid for me
　　within a pit their net;
　which without cause they for my soul
　　have digged and for me set.
8 Upon him let destruction come
　　when he's at unawares,
　and let his net that he hath hid
　　himself catch in its snares;

　Straightway into that very same
　　destruction let him fall:
9 and so from henceforth in the LORD
　　my soul be joyful shall:
　It shall in his salvation great
　　rejoice and thankful be.
10 And all my bones shall say in praise,
　　LORD, who is like to thee,

　The poor man which deliverest
　　from him too strong for him,
　yea, he that poor and needy is
　　from him that spoileth him?
11 False witnesses rose up and stood,
　　and to my charge they laid
　things that I knew not; they 'gainst me
　　false accusation made.

12 They ill for good rewarded me,
    to spoil my soul thereby;
13 but as for me, when they were sick,
    with sackcloth clothed was I.
    Moreover humbled I my soul;
    with fasting I did pray:
    and yet my prayer returned, and thence
    in mine own bosom lay.

14 I did behave as though he'd been
    my friend or brother born:
    I bowed down heavily as one
    doth for his mother mourn.
15 But in mine own adversity
    they did rejoice, for shame;
    together gathered they themselves,
    yea, all the abjects came;

    Together gathered they themselves,
    they 'gainst me did increase:
    I knew it not; yea, they at me
    did tear, and would not cease:
16 With mockers hypocritical
    in feasts, they did on me
17 gnash with their teeth: Lord, how long wilt
    thou look, and silent be?

    My soul from their destructions cruel
    to rescue now draw near,
    my darling from the lions strong
    which ravenous appear.
18 Within the congregation great
    give thanks to thee I will:
    among much people I'll thee praise,
    yea, I will praise thee still.

19 O let not them that are my foes
    joy wrongfully o'er me:
them neither with the eye let wink
    that hate me causelessly.

20 For peace they speak not, but devise
    to work with subtle hand
deceitful matters 'gainst them that
    are quiet in the land.

21 Yea, they against me opened wide
    their mouth, and said this word:
Aha, aha, our eye hath seen.

22   This thou hast seen, O LORD:
Lord, keep not silence: be not far:

23   stir up thyself straightway;
wake to my judgment and my cause,
    my God, my Lord, I pray.

24 According to thy righteousness
    me judge, O LORD my God;
and let them not rejoice o'er me
    that would me harm afford.

25 Let them not say within their hearts,
    Ah, have it so would we:
let them not say, We've swallowed him,
    that he devoured might be.

26 Together let them be ashamed
    and to confusion brought,
that at mine hurt do now rejoice
    and for mine harm have sought.
Let them each one be clothed with shame,
    and with dishonour girt,
that magnify themselves 'gainst me,
    and triumph at my hurt.

27 Let them shout loud for joyfulness,
    and gladly lift the voice,
that favour do my righteous cause,
    and in the same rejoice:
Yea, Let the LORD be magnified,
    let them say constantly,
Which pleasure in his servant hath,
    and his prosperity.

28 Then of thy righteousness and praise
    speak freely shall my tongue,
and mention make thereof with joy
    and gladness all day long.

PSALM 36

To the chief Musician,
A Psalm of David the servant of the LORD.

London New

1 THE wicked man's transgression saith,
    and doth my heart apprise,
that there is not the fear of God
    at all before his eyes:
2 For he in his own eyes himself
    to flatter doth delight,
till his iniquity appear
    as hateful in his sight.

3 His mouth's words are iniquity,
    deceit's with this combined:
and he hath left off to be wise,
    to good he's not inclined.
4 He mischief doth devise abed;
    he makes himself to be

set in a way that is not good;
  abhor not ill doth he.

5 Thy mercy, LORD, is in the heavens;
  thy faithfulness is nigh
6 unto the clouds: thy righteousness
  is like the mountains high;
  Behold, a deep, profound and great,
  thy wondrous judgments be:
  in safety man and beast, O LORD,
  are both preserved by thee.

7 Thy loving-kindness all excels,
  O God, and sweetly springs:
  men's children therefore trust beneath
  the shadow of thy wings.
8 With thy house' fatness satisfied
  abundantly they'll be;
  and thou shalt of the river make
  them drink thy pleasures free.

9 For truly doth the fountain-spring
  of life with thee remain;
  and light we in the light shall see
  that doth to thee pertain.
10 Thy loving-kindness unto them
  continue that thee know;
  and on all those of upright heart
  thy righteousness bestow.

11 Against me let the foot of pride
  not come and mighty prove,
  and do not let the wicked's hand
  me by its strength remove.

12 There workers of iniquity
    are fallen in our eyes;
they are cast down, and never shall
    be able to arise.

PSALM 37

A Psalm of David

Bristol

1 FRET not thyself because of those
    that evil-doers be,
nor envy bear against them that
    do work iniquity.

2 Because they soon shall be cut down
    like to the grass that's mown,
and wither as the fresh green herb
    as soon as it is grown.

3 Thy trust confide thou in the LORD,
    and patiently do good;
and so thou in the land shalt dwell,
    and verily have food.

4 And also in the LORD do thou
    let thy delight abound;
and he shall give thee those desires
    that in thine heart are found.

5 Commit thy way unto the LORD;
    trust also in him still;
he surely shall it bring to pass,
    and thy desire fulfil.

6 And as the light thy righteousness
    bring forth at length shall he;
thy judgment as the noonday clear
    he'll bring forth unto thee.

7 Rest in the LORD, and wait for him;
    wait patiently, I say:
fret not thyself because of him
    who prosp'reth in his way;
Because of that same man who brings
    to pass with enmity
devices which he hath conceived
    in secret wickedly.

8 From anger cease, and wrath forsake;
    no more the same pursue:
fret not thyself in any wise
    that evil thou should'st do.
9 Cut off shall evil-doers be;
    their hope is nothing worth:
but those that wait upon the LORD
    inherit shall the earth.

10 For yet a little while, and then
    the wicked shall not be:
yea, thou'lt his place with diligence
    consider, but not see.
11 The meek inherit shall the earth,
    for them shall he requite;
and they in the abundance shall
    of peace themselves delight.

12 The wicked plots against the just,
    and gnasheth with his teeth.
13 The Lord shall laugh at him: for that
    his coming day he seeth.
14 The wicked have the sword drawn out,
    and bent their bow have they,
to cast the poor and needy down,
    and men of upright way.

15 But that same sword which they have drawn
    shall enter their own heart;
the very bows which they have bent
    shall broken be apart.
16 A little that a righteous man
    hath from his labour reaped
is better than the riches all
    by many wicked heaped.

17 The wicked's arms shall broken be:
    but righteous men the LORD
18 doth yet uphold; the LORD doth all
    the upright's days record:
Their heritage shall ever stand.
19   They'll unashamed abide
the evil time: they'll be in days
    of famine satisfied.

20 But yet the wicked perish shall,
    the LORD's foes they shall all
as lambs' fat be: they shall consume;
    in smoke consume they shall.
21 The wicked borroweth, and he
    it payeth not again:
but mercy doth the righteous show,
    and giveth all his gain.

22 For such as blessed be of him
    the earth inherit shall;
but they shall wholly be cut off
    on whom his curse doth fall.
23 A good man's steps established are
    and ordered by the LORD:
so that the way wherein he walks
    doth him delight afford.

24 Although he fall, yet shall he not
    be cast down utterly:
for him with his own hand the LORD
    upholdeth constantly.
25 I've young been, and am old: I've not
    the righteous seen unfed,
nor yet forsaken, nor have once
    his seed seen begging bread.

26 He's ever merciful, and lends;
    his seed shall blessed be.
27 Depart from ill, do good, and dwell
    for evermore do ye.
28 The LORD loves judgment, and his saints
    forsaketh not in need;
they e'er preserved are: but cut off
    shall be the wicked's seed.

29 The just inherit shall the land,
    and therein ever dwell.
30 The just man's mouth doth wisdom speak;
    his tongue doth judgment tell.
31 Found in his heart is his God's law;
    his steps slide not away.
32 The wicked doth the righteous watch,
    and seeketh him to slay.

33 The LORD him in his hand leaves not;
    nor him condemn will he
34 when he is judged: wait on the LORD;
    his way keep steadfastly:
He shall exalt thee, for that thou
    inherit shalt the land;
what time the wicked are cut off,
    thou'lt see and understand.

35 I have the wicked in great power
   on earth established seen,
   and spreading out himself like as
   a mighty bay-tree green.
36 Yet he did pass, lo, he was not:
   yea, him I sought, but he
37 could not be found: but mark that man,
   the perfect man mark ye:

Behold the upright, for the end
   of that man is in peace.
38 Transgressors soon shall be destroyed,
   together they shall cease:
The latter end shall be cut off
   of wicked men abhorred.
39 But the salvation of the just
   is ordered by the LORD:

For he their strength is in the time
   of trouble and of grief;
40 the LORD shall help and set them free,
   and send to them relief:
He from the wicked evermore
   deliver shall the just,
and shall them save, because by faith
   in him they put their trust.

PSALM 38

A Psalm of David, to bring to remembrance.

Culross

1 IN thy great wrath, I thee beseech,
      O LORD, rebuke me not:
   and neither do thou chasten me
      in thy displeasure hot.

72

2 For in me fast thine arrows stick;
   thy hand doth press me sore.
3 There through thy wrath is in my flesh
   no soundness any more;

And I no rest have in my bones,
   nor any peace within,
because that I am much distressed
   and troubled for my sin.
4 Gone up are mine iniquities,
   above mine head they be:
and as an heavy burden they
   too heavy are for me.

5 My wounds do stink and are corrupt
   for this my foolishness;
6 I am with trouble greatly vexed,
   and bowed in my distress.
Moreover I in mourning go
   and sorrow all day long:
7 my loins are filled with foul disease
   which loathsome is and strong.

There is no soundness in my flesh:
8   I'm feeble, broken sore;
by reason of disquiet of heart
   I have been made to roar.
9 All my desire, O Lord, and hope
   before thee thou dost see;
as to the groaning that I make,
   it is not hid from thee.

10 My heart doth pant, my strength doth fail,
   alas, I am undone:
as for the light that's of mine eyes,
   'tis also from me gone.

11　Aloof, my lovers and my friends
　　　　stand from my sore afar;
　　they also stand far off from me
　　　　that kinsmen to me are.

12　They that seek for my life lay snares:
　　　　those that would do me wrong
　　speak things mischievous, and deceits
　　　　imagine all day long.

13　But as a deaf man heard I not;
　　　　and I was as one dumb:
　　a man that opens not his mouth,
　　　　from whom no words do come.

14　Thus was I even as a man
　　　　that heareth not a sound;
　　and in whose mouth are no reproofs,
　　　　and no reproach is found.

15　For I, O LORD, do all my hope
　　　　repose alone in thee:
　　yea, thou wilt hear, O Lord my God.

16　　　For I did say, Hear me;

　　Lest otherwise they over me
　　　　should with rejoicing cry:
　　when my foot slippeth, they themselves
　　　　against me magnify.

17　For I am ready now to halt,
　　　　and can endure no more;
　　continually my sorrow great
　　　　appeareth me before.

18　For unto thee I will declare
　　　　all mine iniquity;
　　and for the sin that I have done
　　　　I sorrowful will be.

19 But lively are mine enemies,
    and they are strong and great;
and they in number multiply
    that wrongfully me hate.

20 They are mine adversaries that
    for good do render ill,
because the thing that good appears
    I wholly follow still.
21 Forsake me not, O LORD: be not
    far from me, O my God.
22 Lord my salvation, make thou haste,
    and help to me afford.

PSALM 39

To the chief Musician, even to Jeduthun,
A Psalm of David.

Beatitudo

1 I SAID, I'll to my ways take heed,
    lest sin I with my tongue:
my mouth I'll with a bridle keep,
    the wicked whilst among.
2 With silence I was dumb, my peace
    I held, yea, e'en from good;
stirred was my sorrow, I no more
    the good did that I would.

3 My heart thus in me hot became
    and in me sore did ache;
whilst I was musing burned the fire:
    then with my tongue I spake:
4 Make me, O LORD, to know mine end,
    the measure of my days,

just what it is, that I may know
  the frailty of my ways.

5 Lo, thou my days an handbreadth mad'st;
    mine age before thee's nought:
  in truth each man at best estate
    with vanity is fraught.
6 In vain show each man surely walks,
    disquieted in vain;
  he heaps up riches, knowing not
    who'll gather them again.

7 And now, O Lord, what wait I for?
    my hope doth rest in thee.
8 Free me from my transgressions all:
    let fools reproach not me.
9 As dumb, I opened not my mouth,
    because thou'st brought me low.
10 Remove thy stroke away: thine hand
    consumes me by its blow.

11 When with rebukes thou dost correct
    man for iniquity,
  his beauty like a moth consumes:
    for each man's vanity.
12 Attend, and hear my prayer, O Lord,
    give ear unto my cry;
  peace hold not at my tears: with thee
    a stranger here am I;

  I sojourn as my fathers all.
13   O spare and cause thou me
  strength to recover, ere I hence
    depart, no more to be.

PSALM 40

To the chief Musician, A Psalm of David.

Ballerma

1 I WAITED long upon the LORD;
    with patience waited I:
at length he unto me inclined,
    and hearkened to my cry.

2 He me out of a noisome pit
    and miry clay did free,
and on a rock he set my feet:
    my goings stablished he.

3 He put a new song in my mouth,
    e'en praise unto our God:
there many shall it see, and fear,
    and trust shall in the LORD.

4 O blessed is that man whose trust
    upon the LORD relies;
respecting not the proud, nor such
    as turn aside to lies.

5 O LORD my God, full many are
    thy wondrous works of old
which thou hast done, yea, and thy thoughts
    which are to usward told:
They cannot once be reckoned up
    in order unto thee:
if I'd declare and speak, they are
    more than can numbered be.

6 Both sacrifice and offering
    thou didst desire no more;
behold, mine ears thou opened hast,
    for thou mine ears didst bore:

    Both off'ring burnt and that for sin
      thou'st not at all desired;
    yea, off'ring burnt, sin-off'ring thou
      hast surely not required.

7   Then said I therefore, Lo, I come;
      do thou behold and see:
    within the volume of the book
      it written is of me.

8   For I delight to do thy will,
      O thou my God that art:
    yea, that most holy law of thine
      I have within my heart.

9   I've in the congregation great
      preached righteousness: and, lo,
    I never have refrained my lips,
      O LORD, as thou dost know.

10 Thy righteousness within my heart
      not hidden once have I:
    I have declared thy faithfulness
      and thy salvation nigh:

    Thy loving-kindness and thy truth
      I surely have revealed;
    them from the congregation great
      I never have concealed.

11 Thy tender mercies sure, O LORD,
      withhold not thou from me:
    let loving-kindness thine and truth
      preserve me constantly.

12 For ills past number compassed me:
      yea, hold upon me took
    all mine iniquities, so that
      I cannot upward look;

They more than hairs are of mine head:
    hence is mine heart dismayed.
13 Be pleased, LORD, to deliver me:
    LORD, hasten to mine aid.

14 Let all that would my soul destroy
    shamed and confounded be;
  let them be driven back and shamed
    that evil wish to me.

15 For sure reward of this their shame,
    let them be cast away
  in desolation that to me,
    Aha, aha, do say.

16 Let all those that thee seek rejoice
    and glad in thee abide:
  who thy salvation love say still,
    The LORD be magnified.
17 I'm poor and needy, yet the Lord
    upon me thought doth take:
  my help thou and deliv'rer art;
    my God, no tarrying make.

PSALM 41

To the chief Musician, A Psalm of David.

Kilmarnock

1 HE blessed is that doth the poor
    consider, for the LORD
  in time of trouble will to him
    deliverance afford.
2 The LORD will him preserve and keep,
    that he may safely live;
  and on the earth his blessing he
    will to him surely give:

And thou wilt not deliver him
 unto his en'mies' will.
3 Him on the bed of languishing
 the LORD will strengthen still:
Thou'lt all his bed in sickness make.
4 I said, LORD, unto me
be merciful and heal my soul;
 for I have sinned 'gainst thee.

5 Mine enemies do evil speak,
 and would me put to shame:
When shall he die, of me they say,
 that perish may his name?
6 Comes he to me, his speech is vain:
 iniquity his heart
doth gather to itself; he goes
 abroad, it to impart.

7 All that me hate together join
 and 'gainst me whisper lies:
against me they as one conspire,
 and do my hurt devise.
8 To him, they say, there cleaveth fast
 an ill disease and sore:
and now that he doth lie, behold,
 he shall rise up no more.

9 Yea, and mine own familiar friend,
 in whom confide did I,
which of my bread did eat, his heel
 'gainst me hath lifted high.
10 But thou, O LORD, do thou to me
 be merciful, I pray;
and do thou raise me up again,
 that them requite I may.

11 By this I know that surely thou
    dost favour to me show,
because o'er me mine enemy
    doth not in triumph go.

12 And as for me, thou me uphold'st
    in mine integrity,
and evermore before thy face
    thou settest me to be.

13 Of Isr'el bless'd the LORD God be,
    from everlasting, then
to everlasting ages all:
    Amen, yea, and Amen.

PSALM 42

To the chief Musician,
Maschil, for the sons of Korah.

Spohr

1 AS pants the hart for water-brooks
    in thirsty lands and dry,
so after thee my longing soul,
    O God, doth pant and cry.

2 For God, yea, for the living God,
    my soul doth thirst in me:
when shall my longing soul come near,
    and in God's presence be?

3 By day my tears have been my meat,
    at night I weep and pray;
while unto me continually,
    Where is thy God? they say.

4 When I remember do these things,
    and meditate thereon,
in me my soul's outpoured: for with
    the multitude I'd gone;

I with the voice of joy and praise
    to God's house went, I say,
with them, e'en with a multitude,
    that did keep holyday.
5 O why art thou cast down, my soul?
    and why, with grief outpoured,
art thou disquieted in me?
    put thou thy hope in God:

For I'll yet praise him for the help
    his count'nance doth bestow.
6 O thou my God, my soul's cast down
    and brought within me low:
Now therefore oft from Jordan's land
    remember thee I will,
from far lands of the Hermonites,
    and from the Mizar hill.

7 When sound thy waterspouts aloud,
    deep unto deep doth call:
gone over me are all thy waves,
    on me thy billows fall.
8 The LORD his loving-kindness will
    command in time of day;
his song's with me by night: I'll to
    the God of my life pray.

9 I'll say to God my rock, Why me
    hast thou forgotten so?
and for the foe's oppression cruel,
    why do I mourning go?
10 As with a sword thrust in my bones,
    my foes reproach each one;
while daily unto me they say,
    Where is thy God now gone?

11 O why art thou cast down, my soul?
    and why, with grief outpoured,
art thou disquieted in me?
    put thou thy hope in God:
For yet I shall give praise to him,
    who ever unto me
the health is of my countenance:
    behold, my God is he.

PSALM 43

There is a Fountain + refrain

1 JUDGE me, and plead my cause against
    a godless folk, O God:
from the deceitful man unjust
    deliv'rance me afford.
2 For thou the God art of my strength:
    why cast me from thee so?
and for the foe's oppression cruel,
    why do I mourning go?

3 O send thy light out and thy truth:
    let them me lead on high
and bring me to thy holy hill,
    thy tabernacles nigh.
4 Then will I to God's altar go,
    God my exceeding joy:
yea, thee to praise, O God my God,
    I will the harp employ.

5 O why art thou cast down, my soul?
    and why, with grief outpoured,
art thou disquieted in me?
    put thou thy hope in God:

For yet I shall give praise to him,
    who ever unto me
the health is of my countenance:
    behold, my God is he.

PSALM 44

To the chief Musician
for the sons of Korah, Maschil.

Kingsfold

1 WE with our ears have heard, O God,
      our fathers have us told,
what work thou in their days didst work,
    e'en in the times of old.

2 How thou didst drive the heathen out,
    and plant'st them with thine hand;
how thou the people didst afflict
    and cast them from the land.

3 For in possession got they not
    the land by their own sword;
their own arm neither unto them
    salvation did afford:
But thy right hand, and thine arm saved;
    thy countenance alone
gave light to them, because thou hadst
    a favour to thine own.

4 Because thou art my King, O God,
    deliv'rances command
5 for Jacob: through thee we'll push down
    our foes that 'gainst us stand:
We through thy name will tread down those
    that 'gainst us risen be.

6 My bow I'll trust not, and my sword
    no safety brings to me.

7 Thou'st saved us from our foes, and hast
    our haters put to shame.
8 In God we boast the whole day long,
    and ever praise thy name.
9 But now, alas, thou'st cast us off,
    and put to shame are we;
    and in their going forth our hosts
    forsaken are by thee.

10 Thou dost us from the enemy
    make backward turn away:
    and they that hatred bear to us
    take for themselves the prey.
11 Like sheep thou hast us given that
    for meat appointed are;
    and 'mong the heathen nations all
    thou hast us scattered far.

12 Thou dost thy people sell for nought,
    (yea, this doth thee suffice;)
    and thou dost not increase at all
    thy wealth by this their price.
13 Unto our neighbours a reproach
    we have been made by thee,
    a scorn and a derision great
    to them that round us be.

14 Among the heathen thou dost us
    a byword also make;
    among the people thou'st us made
    a cause the head to shake.
15 Before me my confusion deep
    abides continually,
    and of my countenance the shame
    hath also covered me,

16 E'en for his voice that doth reproach,
   and blasphemy doth speak;
   by reason of the enemy
   that doth for vengeance seek.

17 All this is on us come, and yet
   we've not forgotten thee,
   and neither in thy covenant
   with falsehood dealt have we.

18 Our heart is not turned back, our steps
   have from thy way not strayed;

19 though us thou'st rent in dragons' place,
   and in death's shadow laid.

20 If we God's name forgot, or stretched
   to a strange God our hands;

21 shall not God search this out? for he
   heart's secrets understands.

22 Yea, altogether for thy sake
   killed all day long are we:
   as sheep unto the slaughter sent
   we counted are by thee.

23 Awake, awake for us, O Lord,
   why sleepest thou, we pray?
   arise, and evermore from thee
   do not us cast away.

24 O wherefore dost thou far from us
   thy countenance withdraw,
   and our affliction dost forget,
   and our oppression sore?

25 Our soul's bowed down to dust, our bowels
   hold on the earth do take.

26 Rise for our help, and us redeem,
   e'en for thy mercies' sake.

PSALM 45

To the chief Musician upon Shoshannim, for
the sons of Korah, Maschil, A Song of loves.

Nearer Home (short metre)

1 O HEARKEN, for my heart
    good matter doth indite:
I speak the things which I have made,
    and of the king do write.
A ready writer's pen
    my tongue doth me afford:
2 Thou fairer than men's children art,
    grace in thy lips is poured;

God hath thee ever bless'd.
3   Thy sword gird on thy thigh,
most mighty, with thy glory bright,
    and majesty on high.
4 And in thy majesty
    ride prosp'rously alway
for truth and meekness, righteousness:
    O prosper in thy way!

Thy right hand shall thee teach
5   things terrible: to bring
thine arrows sharp within the heart
    of en'mies of the king;
Whereby the people fall
    defeated under thee.
6 Thy throne, O God, for ever is,
    and evermore shall be:

Thy kingdom's sceptre is
7   a sceptre right. For thou
lov'st righteousness, hat'st wickedness,
    dost equity avow:

And therefore God, thy God,
   hath e'en anointed thee
with oil of gladness far above
   thy fellows all that be.

8 Of aloes, cassia, myrrh,
   thy garments fragrance had,
out of the iv'ry palaces,
   whereby they've made thee glad.

9 Thy women honourable
   were with kings' daughters seen:
and clad in gold of Ophir stood
   on thy right hand the queen.

10 O daughter, hearken thou,
   give thought, thine ear incline:
forget the people once thine own,
   thy father's house and line;

11 So greatly shall the king
   thy beauty fair desire:
he is thy Lord, and worship thou,
   him worship and admire.

12 The daughter fair of Tyre
   there with a gift shall be,
the rich among the people shall
   entreat thy favour free.

13 The daughter of the king
   in glory there is seen,
all glorious within: of gold
   her clothing wrought hath been.

14 Behold, unto the king
   in robes she shall be brought,
her stately raiment glorious
   of needlework is wrought:

And they that follow her,
   them also thou shalt see:
the virgins her companions pure
   shall all be brought to thee.

15 With gladness they'll be brought,
   rejoicing on their way:
into the palace of the king
   their entrance make shall they.

16 Instead of fathers thine
   thou shalt thy children take,
those whom in all the earth abroad
   thou mayest princes make.

17 And I will make thy name
   in generations all
to be remembered: evermore
   the people praise thee shall.

PSALM 46

To the chief Musician for the sons of Korah,
A Song upon Alamoth.
                    S. Anne

1 GOD is our refuge and our strength,
   and doth for us appear
a very present help in need,
   in time of trouble near.

2 We therefore will not fear although
   the earth removed should be,
and though the mountains carried were
   amidst the troubled sea;

3 Although the waters thereof roar,
   and do a tumult make;
though with the swelling seas thereof
   the mountains move and shake.

4 A river is, whose streams make glad
    the city of our God,
the tabernacles' holy place,
    the most High's own abode.

5 For God is in the midst of her,
    and she shall never move:
God unto her an helper shall,
    and that right early, prove.

6 The heathen raged in wrath, and moved
    the kingdoms did appear;
he uttered but his voice: forthwith
    the earth did melt for fear.

7 The LORD of hosts is with us still,
    he ever doth endure;
and Jacob's God our refuge is,
    abiding ever sure.

8 Come, and the LORD's own works behold
    that have destruction brought:
what desolations he hath made,
    and in the earth hath wrought.

9 He to the earth's end makes wars cease,
    destroyed makes bows to be;
he cuts in twain the spear, in fire
    the chariot burneth he.

10 Be still, and know that I am God:
    I'll be exalted high
among the heathen: in the earth
    exalted be will I.

11 The LORD of hosts is with us still,
    he ever doth endure;
and Jacob's God our refuge is,
    abiding ever sure.

PSALM 47

To the chief Musician,
A Psalm for the sons of Korah.

Evangel

1 O CLAP your hands, ye people all,
    and make a joyful noise;
shout unto God and cry to him
    with loud triumphant voice.

2 Because the LORD most high doth rule,
    and terrible is he;
a King high over all the earth,
    and great in majesty.

3 He under us the people shall
    make subject in defeat,
the nations he shall overthrow
    and bring beneath our feet.

4 And for us our inheritance
    he choose shall and secure:
of Jacob, whom he loved of old,
    the excellency sure.

5 God is gone up, and with a shout,
    his praise to magnify.
The LORD's gone with a trumpet's sound,
    with trumpet sounding high.

6 To God sing praises, praises sing,
    sing praises to our King,

7 sing praises: God's King of all earth:
    with knowledge praises sing.

8 God over all the heathen reigns:
    God sitteth on the throne
of his exalted holiness,
    in majesty made known.

9 The princes of the people all
    together gathered are,
e'en of the God of Abraham,
    the people from afar:

For of the earth the mighty shields
    assuredly are his:
they unto God belong, and he
    exalted greatly is.

(repeat verse 1)

PSALM 48

A Song and Psalm for the sons of Korah

S. Magnus

1 GREAT is the LORD, and greatly shall
    they praise to him express
in our God's city, in the mount
    of his own holiness:
2 For situation beautiful,
    the whole earth's joy besides,
the great King's city, Zion's mount,
    set on the northern sides.

3 God in her palaces is known,
    a refuge to us nigh.
4 For, lo, the kings assembled were,
    together passed they by.
5 They saw and marvelled; hasted they,
    for trouble did them ail.
6 Fear took them there, and pain as of
    a woman in travail.

7 For thou didst break up all the ships
    that were from Tarshish sent:

thou with an east wind didst them break,
   and by it they were rent.
8 As we have heard, so have we seen,
   therein 'tis noised abroad,
O city of the LORD of hosts,
   the city of our God:

God stablish it for ever will:
9   we've thought of all thou didst
in loving-kindness free, O God,
   within thy temple's midst.
10 According to thy name, O God,
   so also is thy praise
unto earth's ends: thy right hand's full
   of righteousness always.

11 Let Zion mount rejoice, and glad
   let Judah's daughters be,
because of all the judgments that
   are given forth by thee.
12 Go forth, and Zion walk about,
   go round about her, tell,
O tell ye all the towers thereof,
13   and mark her bulwarks well;

Consider ye her palaces:
   that it in turn may ye
unto the generation tell
   that after you shall be.
14 For ever and for ever doth
   this God our God abide:
he even unto death itself
   will be to us a guide.

Psalm 49

To the chief Musician,
A Psalm for the sons of Korah.

Bristol

1 HEAR this, all people; give ye ear,
    all in the world that dwell.
2 Both low and high, yea, rich and poor,
    together hearken well.
3 My mouth shall of true wisdom speak,
    that hear the same may ye;
  the meditation of my heart
    shall understanding be.

4 I will incline mine ear unto
    a parable profound:
  I open will my saying dark,
    upon the harp to sound.
5 Oh, wherefore should I fear in days
    of evil breaking out;
  or when my heels' iniquity
    shall compass me about?

6 They in their wealth that put their trust,
    and boast themselves with pride
  because of all the riches great
    which they have multiplied,
7 Not one of them by any means
    his brother can redeem,
  nor can he give to God for him
    a ransom he'll esteem:

8 (Their soul's redemption precious is,
    and cease it doth for aye:)
9 that he should still for ever live
    and his corruption stay.

10 That wise men and the fool both die
    he clearly can perceive,
with them the brutish perish: they
    their wealth to others leave.

11 Their inward thought is, that their house
    continue ever shall;
their dwelling-place, they trust, shall last
    to generations all;
They call their lands by their own names.
12   Though man in honour be
yet he abides not: like the beasts
    that perish soon is he.

13 This way of theirs their folly is,
    for swiftly they are gone:
yet their posterity approve
    their sayings every one.
14 Death feed shall on them, when like sheep
    they laid are in the grave;
the upright in the morning shall
    dominion o'er them have;

Their beauty in the grave consumed
    shall from their dwelling be.
15 God from grave's pow'r my soul redeems:
    for me receive shall he.
16 When one is unto riches come,
    then be not thou afraid;
nor when the glory of his house
    much to increase is made;

17 For when he dieth nothing hence
    he carry shall away:
his glory after him shall not
    descend, nor with him stay.

18 Though while he lived he bless'd his soul:
       (for thou men's praise wilt earn
   when to thyself thou doest well.)
19   he shall to dust return;

   And to his fathers he shall go,
       and pass away from sight;
   yea, to the generation where
       they never shall see light.
20 Man that is much in honour found,
       and understands not this,
   though high esteemed 'mong men, yet he
       like beasts that perish is.

PSALM 50

A Psalm of Asaph

S. Bride (short metre)

1 THE mighty God, the LORD,
       spake forth, the earth to call
   from where the sun doth rise to where
       his going down doth fall.
2 From out of Zion high,
       of excellency bright
   and beauty the perfection fair,
       hath God shined forth in light.

3 Behold, our God shall come,
       and shall not silence keep:
   a fire before him shall devour,
       a tempest round him sweep.
4 Unto the heavens high
       he from above shall call,
   and to the earth, that he himself
       may judge his people all.

5 Together let my saints
    unto me gathered be;
those that by sacrifice have made
    a covenant with me.
6 The heavens shall declare
    his righteousness abroad,
for he is judge himself: behold,
    there is no judge but God.

7 My people, hear, I'll speak;
    and I will testify
and 'gainst thee plead, O Israel:
    God, e'en thy God, am I.
8 For sacrifices thine
    I'll no reproof give thee,
or thy burnt off'rings, to have been
    before me constantly.

9 No bullock will I take
    from any house of thine,
10 nor he-goats from thy folds, for all
    the forest's beasts are mine.
Upon a thousand hills
    the cattle to me yield.
11 I know all mountains' fowls: and mine
    are wild beasts of the field.

12 And if I hungry were,
    thee I would never tell,
because the world itself is mine,
    and all that therein dwell.
13 Will I eat flesh of bulls,
    or goats' blood drink will I?
14 Thanksgiving offer unto God;
    pay vows to the most High:

15 And on me in the day
      of trouble do thou call:
   I'll thee deliver, and by thee
      be glorified I shall.
16 God to the wicked saith,
      Why dost thou undertake
   my statutes to declare, or in
      thy mouth my cov'nant take?

17 Yea, seeing that thou dost
      instructed hate to be,
   and that thou dost behind thy back
      cast all my words from thee.
18 With him consentedst thou,
      when thou a thief hadst seen;
   and thou hast with adulterers
      partaker also been:

19 To ill thou giv'st thy mouth,
      deceit thy tongue to frame:
20 thou sitt'st and 'gainst thy brother speak'st,
      thy mother's son dost shame.
21 These things thou'st surely done;
      I silence kept till now:
   thou thought'st that altogether I
      was such an one as thou:

   But I will thee reprove,
      and yet before thine eyes
   these things I will in order set,
      confounding all thy lies.
22 Now, ye that God forget,
      consider this with care;
   lest, when there no deliv'rer is,
      I you in pieces tear.

23 Whoso doth offer praise
    me glorifieth so;
to him that orders right his way
    I'll God's salvation show.

PSALM 51

To the chief Musician, A Psalm of David,
when Nathan the prophet came unto him,
after he had gone in to Bath-sheba.

Selma (short metre)

1 UPON me mercy have,
    and do thou pity me,
according to thy grace, O God,
    and loving-kindness free:
Blot my transgressions out,
    and unto me incline,
according to the multitude
    of tender mercies thine.

2 From mine iniquity
    me throughly wash within,
yea, do thou wash me utterly
    and cleanse me from my sin.

3 For my transgressions I
    acknowledge unto thee;
my sin before me ever is:
    my fault I ever see.

4 Against thee, only thee,
    I do confess and own,
I sinned have, and this evil great
    done in thy sight alone:

That so, when thou dost speak,
  thou justified might'st be;
and that thou might'st be wholly clear
  what time thou judgest me.

5 Lo, in iniquity
    I shapen was within;
  my mother also at the first
    did me conceive in sin.

6 Thou in the inward parts
    of truth desirous art:
  and wisdom thou shalt make me know
    within the hidden part.

7 With hyssop purge thou me;
    I cleanliness shall know:
  do thou me wash, and then I shall
    be whiter than the snow.

8 Of joy and gladness great
    make me to hear the voice,
  that so the very bones which thou
    hast broken may rejoice.

9 Thy face hide from my sins;
    from them turn thou away:
  all mine iniquities blot out,
    and cover them, I pray.

10 Create, O God, in me
     a clean unblemished heart:
   a spirit that is right renew
     within the inmost part.

11 O let me not far off
     cast from thy presence be;
   nor yet thy holy spirit true
     take thou away from me.

12 Thine own salvation's joy
    do thou to me restore;
and with thy spirit free do thou
    uphold me evermore.

13 Then will I teach thy ways
    unto transgressors all;
and sinners unto thee shall turn,
    and be converted shall.

14 From guiltiness of blood
    do thou deliver me,
O God, who only art the God
    of my salvation free:

Then shall my tongue aloud
    sing of thy righteousness:
15 Lord, open thou my lips: so shall
    my mouth thy praise express.

16 For sacrifice dost thou
    no more at all desire,
else I'd it give: delight'st thou not
    in off'ring burnt by fire.

17 God's sacrifices are
    a broken spirit poor:
a broken and a contrite heart,
    O God, thou'lt not abhor.

18 In thine own pleasure good,
    do good to Zion still;
the walls about Jerusalem
    build up of thy good will.

19 Pleased shalt thou be when they
    the sacrifices bring
of righteousness, with off'ring burnt,
    and whole burnt offering:

This shall thee pleasure give,
  for they shall thee extol:
then shall they offer bullocks slain
  upon thine altar whole.

PSALM 52

To the chief Musician, Maschil, A Psalm of
David, when Doeg the Edomite came and told
Saul, and said unto him, David is come to the
house of Ahimelech.

Dalehurst

1 WHY boast'st thyself, O mighty man,
     in mischief so secure?
God's goodness doth continually
  through ages all endure.
2 Thy tongue deviseth mischiefs like
  a razor sharpened well
3 that works deceitfully. Thou lov'st
  ill more than good to tell;

Thou rather lov'st to lie than speak
4 in righteousness. Thou dost
love all devouring words, O thou
  deceitful tongue unjust.
5 God likewise shall for evermore
  destruction bring on thee:
take thee away and pluck thee from
  thy dwelling-place shall he;

Out of the land of those that live
  he shall thee root straightway.
6 The righteous shall it see and fear,
  and laugh at him shall they:

7 Lo, this man made not God his strength;
    but put his trust did he
in riches great, and made himself
    in mischief strong to be.

8 But like a fresh green olive-tree
    in God's house found am I:
and in God's mercy evermore
    my confidence doth lie.
9 And I for ever will thee praise,
    because thou hast it done:
and on thy name I'll wait; 'tis good
    before thy saints each one.

PSALM 53

To the chief Musician upon Mahalath,
Maschil, A Psalm of David.

Martyrs

1 THE fool hath spoken in his heart,
    There is no God, saith he.
Corrupt, abominably they
    have wrought iniquity:
And there is none that doeth good.
2   From heaven high God viewed
and on men's children looked to see
    if any understood:

Was there but one that did seek God?
3   Each one is backward gone:
they altogether filthy are;
    none do'th good, no, not one.
4 Have workers of iniquity
    no knowledge gained at all?
for they my people eat as bread:
    on God they do not call.

5 There were they in great fear, though they
  no cause of fear could see:
for God hath scattered all the bones
  of him that camped 'gainst thee:
Thou hast them put to shame, for God
  hath them despised to hear.
6 Oh that salvation out of Zion
  to Isr'el would appear!

When back God doth his people bring
  from sore captivity,
then Jacob shall rejoice at last,
  and Isr'el glad shall be.

PSALM 54

To the chief Musician on Neginoth, Maschil,
A Psalm of David, when the Ziphims came
and said to Saul, Doth not David hide himself
with us?

S. Flavian

1 BY thine own name me save, O God,
  and judge me by thy strength.
2 Hear thou my prayer, O God; give ear
  to my mouth's words at length.
3 For strangers ill are risen up
  and do me sore beset;
oppressors seek my soul, and God
  before them have not set.

4 Behold, God is mine helper sure,
  the Lord is with them still
5 that do uphold my soul; he shall
  reward my foes with ill:

Them do thou in thy truth cut off.
6   To thee I freely would
give sacrifice: I'll praise thy name,
O LORD, for it is good.

7 He out of all my trouble hath
me freed and given ease:
and his desire mine eye hath seen
upon mine enemies.

PSALM 55

To the chief Musician on Neginoth,
Maschil, A Psalm of David.

Rest

1 DO thou to me give ear, O God,
when unto thee I pray;
and from my supplication's voice
hide not thyself away.

2 Be thou attentive unto me,
and hearken to my cry:
in my complaint I mourn aloud,
and make a noise do I;

3 Because the en'my's voice doth sound;
because the wicked all
oppress my soul: and on me cause
iniquity to fall;
For in their wrath they do me hate.

4   My heart's sore pained in me:
behold, of death the terrors dread
upon me fallen be.

5 Upon me cometh fearfulness,
and trembling doth me take,
so that with horror overwhelmed
continually I shake.

6 And so I said, Oh that I'd wings
    like to a dove on high!
  for then I'd fly far, far away,
    and be at rest would I.

7 Lo, far I'd wander and within
    the wilderness abide:
8 I'd haste to 'scape the windy storm,
    and from the tempest hide.
9 Destroy, O Lord, divide their tongues,
    that have for tumult been:
  for violence and strife have I
    within the city seen.

10 Upon the walls thereof do they
    go day and night around:
  there mischief also in the midst
    and misery are found.
11 Yea, in the very midst thereof
    doth wickedness appear;
  and from deceitfulness and guile
    her streets are never clear.

12 For 'twas no foe that me reproached;
    then suffer it could I:
  nor yet my hater that 'gainst me
    himself did magnify;
  Then had I hid myself from him:
13   but it was thou, so near,
  a man mine equal, and my guide,
    and mine acquaintance dear.

14 We counsel sweet together took,
    and walked upon the way,
  unto the house of God we went
    in company to pray.

15 Let death upon them seize, and quick
    let them go down to hell:
for wickedness is in their tents,
    and 'mong them where they dwell.

16 But as for me, on God I'll call;
    the LORD me saves from ill.
17 At evening, morn and noon I'll pray,
    and cry aloud I will:
18 He'll hear my voice. My soul in peace
    he freed hath from the war
that was against me: for with me
    there were in number more.

19 God hearken shall, and them afflict:
    of old abideth he.
They therefore fear not God because
    they do not changes see.
20 He hath put forth his hands 'gainst such
    as with him be at peace:
he broken hath his covenant,
    and made the same to cease.

21 More smooth than butter his mouth's words,
    but in his heart was war:
more soft than oil his words, they proved
    drawn swords that wounded sore.
22 Thy burden cast upon the LORD,
    and thee sustain shall he:
behold, he never suffer shall
    the righteous moved to be.

23 But thou, O God, shalt bring them down,
    and they shall surely fall;
yea, thou into destruction's pit
    shalt swiftly bring them all:

Such bloody and deceitful men
   their hope shall never see,
they shall not live out half their days;
   but I will trust in thee.

PSALM 56

To the chief Musician upon Jonath-elem-
rechokim, Michtam of David, when the
Philistines took him in Gath.

S. Frances

1 BE merciful to me, O God,
   for in my sore distress
man would devour me; he each day
   me fighting doth oppress.

2 Each day devour me would my foes,
   that 'gainst me multiply:
for they against me many be
   that fight, O thou most High.

3 What time I am afraid, in thee
   my trust I will repose.

4 In God I'll praise his word, in God
   I've trusted 'midst my foes;
I therefore will not fear at all
   what flesh can do to me.

5 Each day they wrest my words: their thoughts
   'gainst me for evil be.

6 Together gather they themselves,
   they hide themselves from sight,
they mark my steps, while for my soul
   they wait both day and night.

7 But shall they by iniquity
   escape or flee abroad?

The people in thine anger great
  do thou cast down, O God.

8 Thou tellest all my wanderings,
  upon them thou dost look:
into thy bottle put my tears:
  are they not in thy book?
9 When unto thee I make my cry,
  mine enemies shall be
at once turned back: and this I know;
  for God is still for me.

10 In God his word I'll praise: I will
  his word praise in the LORD.
11 I'll fear not what man do'th to me,
  for I do trust in God.
12 Thy vows, O God, upon me are:
  I'll praises give to thee.
13 For even from the dust of death
  my soul thou hast set free:

From falling wilt thou not my feet
  deliver, and me stay:
that in the light of those that live
  before God walk I may?

PSALM 57

To the chief Musician, Al-taschith, Michtam
of David, when he fled from Saul in the cave.

S. Columba

1 BE merciful to me, O God,
    be merciful to me:
because my soul with confidence
  doth wholly trust in thee:

For in the shadow of thy wings
    I will my refuge make,
till these calamities be past
    that now me overtake.

2 I'll cry to God who is most high,
    and to him make my plea;
yea, I to God will call that doth
    perform all things for me.

3 From heav'n he'll send to save, and me
    from his reproach defend
that would me swallow: mercy forth
    God with his truth shall send.

4 My soul is found among the lions:
    I e'en among them lie
that set on fire are: e'en among
    the sons of men am I;
Whose teeth are spears and arrows cruel
    which do me harm afford;
their tongue doth also sorely wound
    like to a sharpened sword.

5 Be thou, O God, exalted far
    above the heavens high;
yea, over all the earth do thou
    thy glory magnify.

6 They've for my steps prepared a net;
    my soul's bowed down in me:
before me they have digged a pit:
    they 'midst it fallen be.

7 My heart is firmly fixed, O God,
    my heart is fixed, I say:

8 I'll sing and praise: my glory, wake;
    wake, psalt'ry, harp, to play:

9 I'll early wake myself. O Lord,
    I praise to thee will bring
among the people: I'll to thee
    among the nations sing.

10 For to the very heavens high
    thy mercy's great and free:
and even to the clouds above
    doth reach thy verity.
11 Be thou, O God, exalted far
    above the heavens high:
yea, over all the earth do thou
    thy glory magnify.

PSALM 58

To the chief Musician, Al-taschith,
Michtam of David.

Lloyd

1 O CONGREGATION, do ye speak
    in righteousness indeed?
or do ye once, ye sons of men,
    with judgment just proceed?
2 Yea, ye in heart work wickedness,
    and evil ye applaud;
ye weigh the violence of your hands
    in all the earth abroad.

3 The wicked surely are estranged
    ere from the womb they're drawn:
they, speaking lies, do go astray
    as soon as they be born.
4 Like to a serpent's poison ill
    their poison doth appear:

111

they're like the adder deaf that is
    adept to stop her ear;

5 Which will not hearken to the voice
    that charmers sound with skill:
though charming ne'er so wisely, yet
    she will not hear them still.
6 The teeth of every one of them
    break in their mouth, O God:
the great teeth of the lions young
    do thou break out, O Lord.

7 Let them as waters melt away,
    continually which flow:
his arrows cut in pieces when
    to shoot he bends his bow.
8 And as a snail which melts, so let
    them pass away each one:
like woman's birth untimely, that
    they may not see the sun.

9 Before your pots can feel the thorns,
    he shall them take away
as with a whirlwind, both alive,
    and, in his wrath, straightway.
10 The righteous shall rejoice what time
    he doth the vengeance see:
he shall his feet wash in the blood
    of those that wicked be.

11 So, Verily, a man shall say,
    the just have a reward:
he's verily on earth a God
    that judgment doth afford.

PSALM 59

To the chief Musician, Al-taschith, Michtam
of David; when Saul sent, and they watched
the house to kill him.

Lynton

1 MY God, from all mine enemies
    to me deliv'rance send:
from them that up against me rise
    my soul do thou defend.

2 From workers of iniquity
    with speed deliver me,
and do thou save me from those men
    of bloody cruelty.

3 They for my soul lay wait: the strong
    are met with one accord
'gainst me; not for transgression mine,
    nor for my sin, O LORD.

4 They run and do prepare themselves
    who find no fault in me:
awake to help me, and behold,
    and mine affliction see.

5 Awake! LORD God of hosts, the God
    whom Isr'el doth confess,
to visit heathen all: spare none
    that wickedly transgress.

6 Lo, they at eventide return:
    they grudge and make a sound
like to a dog; and forth they go
    about the city round.

7 Behold, they belch out with their mouth
    and make a hateful noise:
set in their lips are swords: For who,
    say they, doth hear our voice?

113

8 But thou, O LORD, shalt laugh at them;
      all heathen thou'lt deride.
9 Because he's strong I'll wait on thee:
      God's my defence most tried.

10 The God that of my mercy is
      shall me prevent and free:
     God shall upon mine enemies
      me my desire let see.
11 Lest that my people should forget,
      them slay not: by thy strength
     and pow'r them scatter; bring them down,
      O Lord our shield, at length.

12 For their mouth's sin and their lips' words
      do thou them take and try
     in this their pride: and for their speech
      in which they curse and lie.
13 In wrath consume them, them consume,
      that they no more may be:
     and that in Jacob God doth rule
      to earth's ends let them see.

14 Let them at eventide return:
      and let them make a sound
     like to a dog; and let them go
      about the city round.
15 And let them wander up and down
      in search of this their meat,
     and let them grudge unsatisfied
      without enough to eat.

16 But I'll thy pow'r sing; I at morn
      sing loud thy mercy will:
     thou'st my defence and refuge been
      in time of trouble ill.

17 O thou who art my strength alone,
     I'll gladly sing to thee:
for God is my defence, the God
     of mercy unto me.

Psalm 60

To the chief Musician upon Shushan-eduth,
Michtam of David, to teach; when he strove
with Aram-naharaim and with Aram-zobah,
when Joab returned, and smote of Edom in
the valley of salt twelve thousand.

Horsley

1 O GOD, thou'st cast us off, thou hast
     us scattered with disdain,
thou'st been displeased; O turn thyself
     unto us yet again.
2 Thou hast the earth to tremble made,
     thou hast it broken sore:
the breaches thereof heal, because
     it shaketh more and more.

3 Thou hast thy people showed hard things,
     things bitter shown to thine:
and thou hast of astonishment
     made us to drink the wine.
4 And thou a banner given hast
     to them that do thee fear,
that for the cause of thine own truth
     displayed it may appear.

5 That thy beloved, whom thou'st loved,
     deliverance may see;
O do thou save with thy right hand,
     and hearken unto me.

115

6 God spake forth in his holiness:
   Rejoicing I'll prevail,
 Shechem by lot will I divide,
   and mete out Succoth's vale.

7 For Gilead is mine; yea, mine
   Manasseh proves to be;
 Ephraim is of mine head the strength;
   law Judah gives by me;
8 My wash-pot Moab is; I will
   o'er Edom cast my shoe:
 because of me, Philistia,
   O do thou triumph too.

9 Who will into the city strong
   me bring with outstretched hand?
 who will me guide upon the way
   that leads to Edom's land?
10 Wilt thou not, O our God, though thou
   hadst cast us off before?
 and thou, O God, which went'st not with
   our armies heretofore?

11 From trouble help us: vain is found
   the help man doth propose.
12 Through God we shall do valiantly:
   he shall tread down our foes.

PSALM 61

To the chief Musician upon Neginah,
A Psalm of David.

Old 18th

1 GIVE ear unto my cry, O God;
   and to my prayer attend.

2 I from the end of all the earth
    my cry to thee will send;
What time my heart is overwhelmed
    and in me low doth lie,
O do thou lead me to the rock
    that higher is than I.

3 Thou hast for me a shelter been,
    a refuge ever near;
a strong tower from the enemy,
    when trouble doth appear.
4 I in thy tabernacle safe
    for ever will abide:
and in the covert of thy wings
    I will my trust confide.

5 For thou, O God, hast heard my vows:
    and thou, who heard'st the same,
hast given me the heritage
    of those that fear thy name.
6 For thou the king's life shalt extend;
    long life thou'lt to him give:
as many generations be
    the years that he shall live.

7 And he before God shall abide,
    and stablished be alway:
O with thy mercy truth prepare,
    which safe preserve him may.
8 So to thy name for evermore
    in song my praise shall be,
that every day I may perform
    the vows made unto thee.

PSALM 62

To the chief Musician, to Jeduthun,
A Psalm of David.

S. Bernard

1 MY soul expecting all day long
doth truly wait on God:
for he it is that unto me
salvation doth afford.

2 Because he only is my rock,
and my salvation free;
he's my defence, and therefore moved
I shall not greatly be.

3 How long will ye against a man
scheme mischief? ye shall all
be slain: for as a wall that bows,
or tott'ring fence, ye'll fall.

4 They only from his excellence
to cast him down converse:
they love to lie; with mouth they bless,
but inwardly they curse.

5 Upon God only wait, my soul,
till he deliv'rance send;
because my expectation doth
on him alone depend.

6 Because he only is my rock,
and my salvation free;
he's my defence, and therefore moved
henceforth I shall not be.

7 In God is my salvation and
my glory's sure abode:
the rock e'en of my strength, besides
my refuge, is in God.

8 Your trust in him at all times place;
    ye people, e'er outpour
your heart before him: God for us
    is still a refuge sure.

9 For surely men are vanity
    that in degree are low;
moreover men of high degree
    are but a lying show:
Together in the balance laid,
    their substance to compare,
they lighter are than vanity,
    yea, lighter than the air.

10 Trust ye not in oppression, nor
    in robbery be vain:
if riches should increase, set not
    your heart upon your gain.

11 For God hath spoken once, yea, twice;
    this have I heard before:
that pow'r belongeth unto God,
    and strength for evermore.

12 And mercy also unto thee,
    O Lord, belongs alone:
for thou according to his work
    dost give to every one.

PSALM 63

A Psalm of David,
when he was in the wilderness of Judah.

Kilsyth

1 O GOD, thou only art my God;
    thee early seek will I:
my soul doth thirst and long for thee,
    my flesh for thee doth cry,

As in a dry and thirsty land,
    where water there is none;
2 to see the pow'r and glory that
    belong to thee alone;

So as I have thee seen before
    within the sanctuary.
3 Thy loving-kindness better is
    by far than life to me;
My lips shall therefore give thee praise:
4   thee also bless will I
whilst I shall live, and in thy name
    I'll lift my hands on high.

5 E'en as with marrow and with fat
    my soul well filled shall be;
so shall my mouth with joyful lips
    give praise aloud to thee:
6 When I remember thee upon
    my bed when fails the light,
and meditate on thee throughout
    the watches of the night.

7 Because thou hast mine helper been,
    and dost sustain me still,
therefore in shadow of thy wings
    rejoice in thee I will.
8 For after thee my earnest soul
    doth follow hard each day:
and for my help thine own right hand
    doth me uphold and stay.

9 Those that my soul seek to destroy
    earth's lower parts shall see.
10 They by the sword shall fall: they shall
    the foxes' portion be.

11 But in God shall the king rejoice,
       and each one glory shall
   that swears by him: but stopped shall be
       the mouth of liars all.

Psalm 64

To the chief Musician, A Psalm of David.

Abbey

1 MY voice, O God, hear in my prayer,
       and my request observe:
   from terror of the enemy
       do thou my life preserve.
2 Me from the secret counsel hide
       of those that wicked be,
   from insurrection of all them
       that work iniquity:

3 Who whet their tongue like to a sword,
       and bend their bows with skill
   to shoot their arrows, even all
       their bitter words and ill:
4 That at the man that perfect is
       in secret shoot they may:
   lo, suddenly they shoot at him,
       and fear no more do they.

5 Themselves they in an evil thing
       encourage wickedly:
   of laying snares they do commune
       in counsel privily.
6 Say they, Who'll see them? They search out
       iniquities all day;
   and with the utmost diligence
       a search accomplish they:

121

Yea, both the secret inward thought
    that every one doth keep,
and of the very heart itself,
    is altogether deep.

7 God shall an arrow shoot at them
    and wound them suddenly.
8 They'll make their tongue fall on themselves:
    all that behold shall flee.

9 All men shall fear, and shall declare
    the work that God hath done;
for of his doing wisely they
    consider shall each one.

10 The just shall in the LORD be glad,
    and in him trust he will;
and all that upright are in heart
    shall glory in him still.

PSALM 65

To the chief Musician,
A Psalm and Song of David.

S. Stephen

1 IN Zion praise doth wait, O God,
    abiding still for thee:
and unto thee the promised vow
    performed shall surely be.
2 O thou that dost incline thine ear
    and unto prayer attend,
all flesh shall unto thee draw near
    from earth's remotest end.

3 Iniquities too strong for me
    prevailed to my dismay:
but as for our transgressions all,
    them shalt thou purge away.

4 Bless'd is the man whom thou dost choose,
    and causest unto thee
so to approach that in thy courts
    he may a dweller be:

We with the goodness of thy house
    shall satisfied remain,
e'en of the holy temple that
    doth unto thee pertain.
5 By things that are most terrible,
    in righteousness made known,
O God of our salvation great,
    thou answer wilt thine own;

Who art the confidence of all
    the ends of earth that be,
and of them also that are found
    far off upon the sea:
6 Which by his strength, as girt with power,
    sets fast the mounts and hills:
7 which noise of seas, noise of their waves,
    and people's tumult, stills.

8 And they in utmost parts that dwell
    fear at thy tokens' voice:
thou mak'st outgoings of the morn
    and evening to rejoice.
9 Earth visit'st thou and wat'rest it:
    thou mak'st it rich to grow
in plenty with God's river which
    doth full of water flow:

When thou for it provided hast,
    corn thou dost them prepare.
10 Thou also dost abundantly
    the ridges water there:

And thou its furrows settle dost:
  with show'rs thou mak'st it soft:
the springing thou dost bless thereof,
  and bless the springing oft.

11 And with thy goodness thou the year
    abundantly dost crown;
  and in thy goings everywhere
    thy paths drop fatness down.
12 On pastures of the wilderness
    they drop with fatness choice:
  behold, the little hills about
    on every side rejoice.

13 The pastures all are clothed with flocks,
    and for a covering
  the vales are clad with corn; for joy
    they shout, they also sing.

Psalm 66

To the chief Musician, A Song or Psalm.

Crediton

1 A JOYFUL noise make, all ye lands,
    to God your voices raise:
2 sing forth the honour of his name,
    and glorious make his praise.
3 Say unto God, How terrible
    thy works thee show to be!
  through thy great pow'r thine en'mies shall
    submit themselves to thee.

4 For worship thee shall all the earth,
    and give to thee acclaim;
  they'll sing to thee, they'll cry aloud,
    and sing unto thy name.

5 Come and behold the works of God,
 his doing also see:
toward the children born of men
 most terrible is he.

6 The sea he into dry land turned,
 a way he did prepare:
they all went through the flood on foot:
 in him rejoiced we there.

7 For ever by his pow'r he rules;
 his eyes the nations try:
let not those that rebellious are
 exalt themselves on high.

8 Ye people, bless our God, and make
 the voice heard of his praise:

9 which holds our soul in life, and which
 our feet from moving stays.

10 For thou'st, O God, us proved and tried,
 as silver's tried and weighed;

11 thou'st in the net us brought, and on
 our loins affliction laid.

12 Thou'st caused men o'er our heads to ride;
 through fire and flood we passed:
but thou into a wealthy place
 hast brought us out at last.

13 I with burnt off'rings to thy house
 will go, my vows to pay,

14 which my lips uttered, my mouth spake,
 when I in trouble lay.

15 Of fatlings sacrifices burnt
 I'll offer unto thee,
with rams' sweet incense; bullocks whole
 with goats mine off'rings be.

16 Come, hear, all that fear God; I'll tell
    what he did for my soul:
17 I with my mouth unto him cried;
    my tongue did him extol.

18 If I iniquity at all
    within my heart regard,
19 the Lord will hear me not, but God
    me verily hath heard;
    He to my prayer's voice did attend:
20   O let God blessed be,
    which hath not turned away my prayer,
    nor mercy kept from me.

PSALM 67

To the chief Musician on Neginoth,
A Psalm or Song.

Argyle

1 GOD unto us be merciful,
    and us to bless incline;
and of his face the brightness cause
    upon us all to shine;
2 That of thy way upon the earth
    the knowledge may abound;
thy saving health 'mong nations all
    to earth's remotest bound.

3 Thee let the people praise, O God;
    let people all thee praise.
4 O let the nations sing for joy
    and gladsome voices raise:
For thou the people righteously
    shalt judge with justice true,

the nations thou upon the earth
  shalt govern and subdue.

5 Thee let the people praise, O God;
  praise thee let people all.
6 Then shall the earth her increase yield;
  God, our God, bless us shall.
7 Yea, God to bless us plenteously
  in favour shall appear:
and so the ends of all the earth
  shall bow to him in fear.

PSALM 68

To the chief Musician,
A Psalm or Song of David.

Martyrs

1 LET God arise: his enemies
  straightway let scattered be;
and let them also that him hate
  before him swiftly flee.
2 As driven smoke, drive them away:
  as fire makes wax to run,
so at God's presence perish let
  the wicked every one.

3 But let the righteous glad appear;
  and let them joyful be
before their God: yea, let them all
  rejoice exceedingly.
4 To God sing, his name's praises sing:
  extol him with your voice
that rides the heav'ns: the LORD's his name:
  before his face rejoice.

5 A father of the fatherless,
 a judge of widows poor,
is God within his holy place,
 his habitation sure.
6 God doth the solitary set
 in fam'lies: he brings out
those bound with chains: but rebels all
 dwell in a land of drought.

7 O God, when thou went'st forth, and didst
 before thy people go,
when through the desert thou didst march,
8 then shook the earth below;
The heavens also shook and dropped,
 and at God's presence fell:
e'en Sinai at God's presence moved,
 the God of Israel.

9 O God, to thine inheritance
 thou sent'st a plenteous rain,
whereby thou, when it weary was,
 didst it confirm again.
10 Thy congregation dwelt therein,
 thou mad'st their dwelling sure:
and of thy goodness thou, O God,
 prepared hast for the poor.

11 Behold, the Lord did give the word:
 great was the company
12 of those that published it. Apace
 did kings of armies flee:
And she at home that tarried long
 did of the spoil divide.
13 Though ye have lien among the pots,
 ye shall not there abide:

For ye shall as a dove's wings be
    o'erlaid with silver bright,
her feathers spread with yellow gold
    that shineth as the light.

14 Behold, when the Almighty rose,
    and scattered kings therein,
then it was as it were all white,
    to Salmon's snow akin.

15 The hill of God is as the hill
    of Bashan; an high hill,
as is the hill of Bashan high:
16   why leap, ye high hills, still?
This is the hill where God himself
    desireth to reside;
yea, he that is the LORD in it
    for ever will abide.

17 God's chariots twenty thousand are,
    of angels thousands strong:
in Sinai, in the holy place,
    the Lord is them among.
18 Thou hast ascended up on high
    and vict'ry hast achieved,
thou'st captive led captivity,
    thou'st gifts for men received:

Yea, for those that rebellious were,
    that 'gainst thee did rebel,
that so the LORD God might himself
    in truth among them dwell.
19 Bless'd be the Lord, who doth each day
    with benefits us load,
yea, even he that unto us
    is our salvation's God.

20 He of salvation is the God,
        that is our God most strong;
    and unto GOD the Lord from death
        the issues do belong.
21 But God shall sorely wound the head
        of such as be his foes,
    the hairy scalp of one that in
        his trespasses still goes.

22 The Lord said, I again will bring
        from Bashan, I again
    will bring my people from the depths
        that to the sea pertain:
23 That in the blood of thine own foes
        to their perpetual shame
    thy foot in vengeance may be dipped,
        thy dogs' tongue in the same.

24 Behold, they have the goings seen
        that were, O God, of thee;
    the goings of my God, my King,
        within the sanctuary.
25 The singers went before, then those
        on instruments that played;
    among them were the damsels that
        with timbrels music made.

26 Within the congregations all
        bless God, and to him sing:
    the Lord e'en from the fountain bless,
        that doth of Isr'el spring.
27 Their ruler, little Benjamin,
        with Judah's princes high,
    their council; and with Zebulun's,
        princes of Naphtali.

28 It is thy God that hath for thee
    thy strength commanded thus:
now strengthen thou, O God, that work
    which thou hast wrought for us.
29 Because thy temple is therein,
    Jerusalem shall be
the place where gifts are brought, there kings
    bring presents unto thee.

30 Upon the spearmen's company
    thy sore rebuke let fall,
upon the multitude of bulls,
    the people's calves withal:
Till every one submit himself
    with silver pieces bright:
the people scatter thou abroad
    in war that take delight.

31 Those that be princes strange shall come
    from out of Egypt's lands;
and soon shall Ethiopia
    to God stretch out her hands.
32 Sing unto God, ye kingdoms all
    throughout the earth abroad;
O give ye voice and sing aloud
    with praises to the Lord:

33 To him that rides on heav'ns of heav'ns,
    which were of old decreed;
lo, he sends out his voice, and that
    a mighty voice indeed.
34 Strength unto God do ye ascribe:
    for over Israel
his excellence abides; his strength
    within the clouds doth dwell.

35 For thou, O God, art terrible,
    exceeding great thy fear;
out of thy holy places thou
    most dreadful dost appear:
The God of Israel it is
    that by his favour free
gives to his people strength and power.
    O let God blessed be.

PSALM 69

To the chief Musician upon Shoshannim,
A Psalm of David.

Vox Dilecti

1 SAVE me, O God: unto my soul
    come in the waters be.
2 I sink in deepest mire, where there
    no standing is for me:
I into waters deep am come,
    where me the floods o'erflow.
3 I weary of my crying am;
    all day I weeping go:

My throat is dried: mine eyes do fail
    while for my God I wait.
4 They more than hairs are of mine head
    that without cause me hate:
They that are wrongfully my foes
    would me destroy and slay;
they mighty are: then I restored
    what I took not away.

5 O God, thou all my foolishness
    dost know and plainly see;
as for my sins, there is not one
    that hidden is from thee.

6 Let none of them, Lord God of hosts,
    that do upon thee wait,
because of me, at any time,
    be shamed or desolate:

Let none of them, O Isr'el's God,
    that follow after thee,
because of me, at any time,
    vexed or confounded be.
7 Because I for thy sake have borne
    reproach and sore disgrace;
I am into confusion brought,
    shame covered hath my face.

8 And I a stranger am become
    unto my brethren near,
an alien unto those that are
    my mother's children dear.
9 Zeal for thine house hath me consumed;
    and their reproaches all
that with derision thee reproached
    did also on me fall.

10 When wept I, and my soul chastised
    with fasting, that was laid
11 to my reproach: my garment coarse
    I also sackcloth made;
To them a proverb I became.
12   Against me speak they wrong
that gravely in the gate do sit;
    I was the drunkards' song.

13 But as for me, my earnest prayer,
    O Lord, is unto thee;
yea, in a time acceptable
    to thee my cry shall be:

133

O God, in all the multitude
  of mercy thine me hear,
and in thine own salvation's truth
  bow down to me thine ear.

14 Out of the mire deliver me;
  from sinking do me keep:
let me be from my haters freed,
  and from the waters deep.

15 Let not the rising water-flood
  me overflow at last,
nor deep me swallow, nor the pit
  on me her mouth shut fast.

16 Since good thy loving-kindness is,
  hear, LORD: to me incline,
according to the multitude
  of tender mercies thine.

17 Thy face ne'er from thy servant hide,
  nor turn away thine ear;
for I in grievous trouble am:
  with speed do thou me hear.

18 O draw thou nigh unto my soul,
  redeem and set it free:
because of all mine enemies,
  do thou deliver me.

19 Thou my reproach hast surely known,
  my shame, and my disgrace:
mine adversaries every one
  appear before thy face.

20 Reproach hath rent my heart; and full
  of heaviness am I:
I looked for some to pity me,
  but there was no man nigh;

For comforters, but none I found.
21 For meat they gave me gall;
   and vinegar they in my thirst
    gave me to drink withal.

22 Their table let become a snare
   that is before them laid:
   and what had for their welfare been,
    let it a trap be made.
23 Their eyes let darkened be, that they
   see not the way to take;
   and do thou also cause their loins
    continually to shake.

24 On them thine indignation pour,
   and of them spare thou none:
   O let thy wrathful anger great
    take hold of them each one.
25 Their habitation let be made
   most desolate by thee;
   and in the tents which they have pitched
    let none a dweller be.

26 For him whom thou hast smitten down
   they persecute alway;
   and to the grief of those whom thou
    hast wounded talk do they.
27 Add thou to their iniquity
   iniquity the more:
   let them into thy righteousness
    come not for evermore.

28 Let them be blotted from the book
   of those that living be,
   and with the righteous let them not
    be written up by thee.

29 But I am poor and sorrowful,
    yea, sorrowful am I:
  let thy salvation come, O God,
    and set me up on high.

30 The name of God I with a song
    assuredly will praise;
  and to exalt him I my voice
    will in thanksgiving raise.

31 This also shall the LORD well please,
    and better be by far,
  than ox or bullock that hath horns,
    and hoofs that cloven are.

32 What time the humble this behold,
    it joy to them shall give:
  all ye that after God do seek,
    your heart shall ever live.

33 Because the LORD regards the poor
    and hearkens to their cries;
  and neither will at any time
    his prisoners despise.

34 Let both the heaven and the earth
    him praise with joyful voice;
  yea, let the seas and everything
    that moves therein rejoice:

35 For God will Zion save, and he
    will Judah's cities raise:
  that they may have their dwelling there,
    and it possess always.

36 His servants' seed it also shall
    inherit from their kin:
  and they that love his name in truth
    shall ever dwell therein.

PSALM 70

To the chief Musician, A Psalm of David,
to bring to remembrance.

Calvary (short metre)

1 DO thou make haste, O God,
     with speed deliver me;
  O make thou haste to help me, LORD,
     and my deliv'rer be.

2 Let them be shamed and vexed
     that 'gainst my soul conspire:
  let them turn back, and be confused,
     that do my hurt desire.

3 Together let them all
     be backward turned away,
  for sure reward of this their shame,
     Aha, aha, that say.

4 Let all that seek thee joy,
     and glad in thee abide:
  who thy salvation love say still,
     Let God be magnified.

5 I poor and needy am:
     O God, haste for my sake;
  my help thou and deliv'rer art:
     O LORD, no tarrying make.

PSALM 71

Redhead No. 66

1 IN thee, O LORD, I put my trust:
     confused let me not be.

2 O do thou in thy righteousness
     with speed deliver me;

Moreover cause me to escape:
    incline to me thine ear;
yea, do thou hearken and me save,
    and for mine aid appear.

3 Be thou my habitation strong,
    whereto I'll e'er resort:
thou gav'st commandment me to save;
    thou art my rock and fort.

4 Out of the wicked's hand, my God,
    do thou deliver me;
from the unrighteous' hand, and from
    the cruel man's, me free.

5 For thou, O Lord God, art my hope,
    to whom I look alone:
thou'rt from my youth my trust, from whence
    thou help to me hast shown.

6 By thee I have been holden up
    e'en from the womb: thou'rt he
that took me from my mother's bowels:
    my praise is e'er of thee.

7 To many I a wonder am,
    but thou'rt my refuge strong.
8 Filled let my mouth be with thy praise,
    thine honour all day long.
9 Cast me not off at such a time
    when old age leaves me frail;
and neither yet forsake me when
    my strength in me doth fail.

10 For those that are mine enemies
    against me speeches make;
and they that for my soul lay wait
    together counsel take:

11 They say, God hath forsaken him:
    him persecute will we
and take him; for there is not one
    to save and set him free.

12 Be thou not far from me, O God,
    but stay thou ever near:
now, O my God, do thou make haste,
    and for my help appear.

13 Confounded and consumed let them
    be made continually,
that in their hatred to my soul
    mine adversaries be;

Let them be covered with reproach
    who do against me speak,
yea, let dishonour on them fall
    that for my hurt do seek.

14 But I in hope and confidence
    will constantly endure;
I also will with joyfulness
    yet praise thee more and more.

15 Thy right'ness and salvation shall
    my mouth show forth all day;
for I know not the numbers that
    remain to pass away.

16 For in the Lord GOD's strength I will
    go on, and not decline:
I mention of thy righteousness
    will make, e'en only thine.

17 O God, up from the time of youth
    by thee I have been taught:
and hitherto I have declared
    the wonders thou hast wrought.

18 Now also when I aged am,
   and have grey-headed grown,
O God, do thou forsake me not,
   nor leave thou me alone;

Till to this generation I
   have showed thy strength aright,
and to each one that is to come
   declared thy pow'r and might.

19 Thy righteousness withal, O God,
   is very high to me,
thou who hast done great things: O God,
   who is like unto thee!

20 Thou, which hast showed me troubles great
   and sore, shalt yet again
me quicken, and from depths of earth
   shalt bring me up again.

21 For thou my greatness surely shalt
   increase yet more and more,
yea, and thou shalt on every side
   be for my comfort sure.

22 I'll also praise thee, e'en thy truth,
   my God, with psaltery:
thou Holy One of Israel,
   with harp I'll sing to thee.

23 For greatly shall my lips rejoice
   when unto thee I sing;
and so my soul, which thou'st redeemed,
   shall praise unto thee bring.

24 And of thy righteousness my tongue
   the whole day long shall speak:
confounded are they, brought to shame,
   that for my hurt do seek.

Psalm 72

A Psalm for Solomon

Effingham

1 GIVE thou, O God, unto the king
    thy judgments every one,
thy righteousness to him that is
    the king's anointed son.
2 And thereupon with righteousness
    thy people judge shall he:
thy poor with judgment he shall rule,
    thine own with equity.

3 Unto the people also peace
    the mountains forth shall bring,
and from the little hills the same
    by righteousness shall spring.
4 He'll of the people judge the poor,
    the needy's children all
he'll save, and the oppressor break
    in pieces very small.

5 Whilst yet the sun and moon endure
    they shall thee fear each one,
henceforth through generations all
    as long as ages run.
6 Like rain upon the new-mown grass
    come down afresh shall he;
as showers that water well the earth
    so his descent shall be.

7 Behold, the righteous in his days
    shall flourish and increase:
and long enduring as the moon
    shall be abundant peace.

8 He shall dominion also have
    from sea to sea afar,
and from the river to the ends
    of all the earth that are.

9 They in the wilderness that dwell
    shall bow before him low;
his enemies shall lick the dust,
    and likewise every foe.
10 The kings of Tarshish, and the isles,
    to him shall presents bring:
and offer gifts to him shall both
    Sheba's and Seba's king.

11 Yea, even all the kings that be
    before him down shall fall:
moreover service do to him
    shall distant nations all.
12 For he deliver shall and free
    the needy when he cries;
withal the poor, and him that hath
    no help in any wise.

13 The poor and needy he shall spare,
    and grant them swift release;
and of the needy he the souls
    shall save, and give them peace.
14 From all deceit and violence cruel
    he shall their soul redeem,
and also precious in his sight
    their blood he shall esteem.

15 And he shall live: of Sheba's gold
    to him shall given be;
for him shall prayer continue, and
    each day be praised shall he.

16 Of corn an handful cast abroad
    shall in the earth be found
upon the top of mountains high,
    in hard and barren ground:

And yet the fruit, like Lebanon,
    shall shake for very worth:
they of the city flourish shall
    like grass upon the earth.

17 His name for ever shall endure:
    his name, just as the sun,
shall long continue: bless'd in him
    shall men be every one:

All nations shall him blessed call:
18   the LORD God blessed be,
the God of Isr'el, who alone
    do'th all things wondrously.

19 And blessed be his glorious name
    for ever. And, again,
his glory let the whole earth fill;
    Amen, yea, and Amen.

20 (Entitled, 'Psalm for Solomon',
    King David's son and heir,
the pleas of David, Jesse's son,
    are ended by this prayer.)

PSALM 73

A Psalm of Asaph

Westminster

1 TO Isr'el truly God is good,
    e'en to those clean of heart.
2 But yet my feet were almost gone:
    my steps did nigh depart.

3 Because that I was envious
    the foolish sort to see,
when I prosperity observed
    in those that wicked be.

4 For in their death there are no bands:
    their strength is firm alway.
5 As others they are troubled not;
    nor like them plagued are they.
6 Pride therefore like unto a chain
    doth compass them around;
and as a garment violence
    is round about them bound.

7 Their eyes stand out with fat: much more
    than heart could wish have they.
8 Corrupt, they of oppression ill
    speak loftily alway.
9 Against the heavens they their mouth
    set in presumptuous talk;
and in their pride their vaunting tongue
    throughout the earth doth walk.

10 His people therefore hither do
    return when this they see:
and waters of a brimming cup
    wrung out unto them be.
11 Because they say, How doth God know,
    how can he it espy?
and is there knowledge of such things
    in him who is most High?

12 Behold, these the ungodly are,
    in all their ways at peace;
who prosper in the world, and they
    in riches much increase.

13 I verily have heretofore
    my heart in vain made clean,
yea, in mine innocence my hands
    most throughly washed have been.

14 For I, alas, have all day long
    been plagued and smitten sore;
and chastened every morning new,
    yea, chastened more and more.

15 But if I say, I will speak thus:
    behold, offend should I
thy children's generation, and
    their grief should multiply.

16 When this I thought to know, I was
    too pained to comprehend:

17 till to God's sanctuary I went,
    and understood their end.

18 For thou in places slippery
    didst surely set them all:
yea, thou into destruction's depths
    didst cast them down to fall.

19 To desolation how are they
    as in a moment brought!
and utterly they are consumed
    with terrors passing thought.

20 And as a dream dismissed when one
    awaketh to arise,
so thou, O Lord, when thou awak'st,
    their image shalt despise.

21 My heart was grieved; pricked in my reins,
    my grief within increased.

22 I foolish was, and ignorant:
    before thee as a beast.

23 I nonetheless do still abide
    continually with thee,
and it is so by my right hand
    that thou hast holden me.

24 Thou shalt me with thy counsel guide,
    and never shalt me leave;
thou'lt lead me on, and afterward
    to glory me receive.

25 In heaven whom have I but thee?
    there is not any one.
And on the earth that I desire,
    beside thee there is none.

26 My flesh and e'en my heart do fail,
    no help from them I draw:
but God the strength is of my heart,
    my portion evermore.

27 They'll perish that are far from thee,
    for thou'lt them overthrow:
thou hast destroyed all them that do
    a-whoring from thee go.

28 But surely it is good for me
    that I to God repair:
I've in the Lord GOD put my trust:
    I'll all thy works declare.

PSALM 74

Maschil of Asaph

Kingsfold

1 O GOD, why hast thou cast us off
    for evermore from thee?
why doth thy wrath smoke 'gainst the sheep
    that of thy pasture be?

2　Thy congregation do thou still
　　in thy remembrance hold,
　the people whom thou purchased hast
　　and called in times of old;

　The rod of thine inheritance,
　　which thou'st thyself redeemed;
　this Zion mount, wherein thou'st dwelt,
　　which was by thee esteemed.
3　Thy feet to desolations lift
　　perpetual that be;
　all that the foe hath wickedly
　　wrought in the sanctuary.

4　Within thy congregations' midst
　　thine enemies do roar;
　and they their ensigns do set up
　　for signs of triumph sure.
5　A man was famous hitherto,
　　and did the people please,
　according as his axes he
　　had lifted on thick trees:

6　But now that work is all destroyed,
　　the carving down they break:
　with axes and with hammers they
　　at once destruction make.
7　They've fire cast in thy sanctuary,
　　defiling all around,
　by casting down the dwelling-place
　　of thy name to the ground.

8　They in their hearts said, Let us them
　　destroy with outstretched hand:

    they all the synagogues of God
      have burned up in the land.
9 Our signs are gone: there is no more
      a prophet to foresee:
    nor 'mong us any that doth know
      how long the time shall be.

10 O God, how long shall us with scorn
      the adversary shame?
    for ever shall the enemy
      blaspheme thy holy name?
11 Why dost thou yet withdraw thy hand,
      yea, e'en thy right hand, thus?
    O from thy bosom pluck it out,
      extend it now to us.

12 For even since the times of old
      God is my King assured,
    salvation working in the midst
      of all the earth abroad.
13 Thou didst divide the sea in twain,
      and there thy strength didst show:
    thou also break'st the dragons' heads
      which in the waters go.

14 Heads of leviathan thou break'st
      in pieces, and didst give
    his meat to people that amidst
      the wilderness do live.
15 Thou clav'st the fountain and the flood:
      thou dri'dst up rivers vast.
16 Both day and night are thine: the light
      and sun prepared thou hast.

17 Thou hast set all the borders fast
    that in the earth exist:
the summer and the winter-time
    thou madest to subsist.
18 Remember that the foe, O LORD,
    did us reproach and shame;
and that the foolish people have
    blasphemed thy holy name.

19 The soul of thine own turtle-dove
    let not delivered be
unto the multitude of those
    that rise up wickedly:
Moreover do thou not forget
    the number of thy poor;
the congregation of the same
    remember evermore.

20 Respect have to the covenant:
    for earth's dark places be
full of the habitations dread
    of hidden cruelty.
21 O therefore let not the oppressed
    return again in shame:
let those that poor and needy are
    give praise unto thy name.

22 Arise, O God, plead thine own cause,
    no more do thou delay:
remember how the foolish man
    reproacheth thee each day.
23 Forget thou not the voice of those
    thine enemies that be:
their tumult that against thee rise
    increaseth constantly.

PSALM 75

To the chief Musician, Al-taschith,
A Psalm or Song of Asaph.

French

1 TO thee, O God, do we give thanks,
   we do give thanks to thee:
because that near thy wondrous works
   declare thy name to be.

2 What time the congregation great
   from thee I shall receive,
with uprightness I then shall judge,
   and unto justice cleave.

3 The earth and all inhabitants
   that unto it belong
are quite dissolved: of it do I
   bear up the pillars strong.

4 Deal ye not now so foolishly,
   unto the fools said I:
and to the wicked I did say,
   Lift not the horn on high:

5 Lift not your horn on high: speak not
   with stiff neck nor proud mouth.

6 Promotion cometh not from east,
   nor west, nor from the south.

7 But God's the judge: he puts down one
   and sets another up.

8 For in the hand that's of the LORD,
   of red wine is a cup;

'Tis full of mixture, of the same
   he pours: the dregs shall all
the wicked of the earth wring out,
   and drink them up they shall.

9 But I'll for evermore declare,
    and praises sing will I
unto the God of Jacob great,
    his name to magnify.

10 I'll also all the wicked's horns
    cut off and cast from me;
but of the righteous all the horns
    exalted high shall be.

PSALM 76

To the chief Musician on Neginoth,
A Psalm or Song of Asaph.

Jackson

1 IN Judah God is known, his name
    is great in Israel.
2 In Salem also is his tent,
    in Zion he doth dwell.
3 There arrows of the bow he brake,
    the shield, the sword, the war.
4 Than mounts of prey, thou dost to us
    excel in glory more.

5 Those that were stout of heart are spoiled,
    the sleep they slept was sound:
and of the men of might none have
    their hands in battle found.
6 When thou, O God of Jacob, them
    rebuked in anger hast,
the chariot and horse are both
    into a dead sleep cast.

7 Thou, even thou, art to be feared:
    and who may in thy sight

stand forth when once thou angry art,
 and risen up in might?
8 Thou judgment mad'st from heaven heard;
 earth feared, and stillness fell,
9 when God to judgment rose, to save
 the meek on earth that dwell.

10 Assuredly the wrath of man
 shall praise give unto thee:
and all that doth remain of wrath
 by thee restrained shall be.
11 Vow, pay ye to the LORD your God:
 let all about him near
come round, and presents bring to him
 that should be held in fear.

12 For he the spirit shall cut off
 of those that princes be:
and to the kings of all the earth,
 lo, terrible is he.

PSALM 77

To the chief Musician, to Jeduthun,
A Psalm of Asaph.

Elgin

1 I UNTO God cried with my voice,
 when trouble did appear;
yea, I to God cried with my voice,
 and he to me gave ear.
2 What day I troubled was, the Lord
 I sought: my sore did run
throughout the night, and did not cease:
 my soul did comfort shun.

3 I God recalled, and troubled was
    with grief exceedingly:
  I did complain, and overwhelmed
    my spirit was in me.
4 For thou mine eyes dost waking hold,
    whilst I for rest do seek:
  I am so vexed with trouble that
    I can no longer speak.

5 I in distress considered have
    the days that were of old,
  the bygone years of ancient times,
    of which our fathers told.
6 I in the night my song recall:
    communion I do take
  with mine own heart: my spirit search
    with diligence did make.

7 For ever will the Lord cast off?
    and favour show no more?
8 clean is his mercy gone? and fails
    his promise evermore?
9 Hath God indeed his gracious word
    forgotten to fulfil?
  and are his tender mercies kind
    shut up in anger still?

10 Said I, 'Tis mine infirmity:
    but yet recall will I
  the former years of his right hand
    who only is most High.
11 I will the LORD's works every one
    in my remembrance hold:
  yea, surely I remember will
    thy wonders done of old.

12 I also will from all thy work
    my meditation draw,
and of the deeds I'll talk which thou
    performed hast heretofore.
13 The way, O God, that thou dost take
    is in the sanctuary:
what God so great is, that he may
    compared with our God be?

14 Thou art the God that wonders great
    dost work with mighty hand:
thou hast declared thy strength among
    the people of the land.
15 And thou thy people with thine arm
    redeemed hast from afar,
of Jacob, and of Joseph, those
    the chosen sons that are.

16 The waters did thee see, O God,
    the waters did thee see;
they were afraid: withal the depths
    were troubled sore by thee.
17 The clouds did pour out water-floods:
    the skies sent out a sound:
thine arrows also went abroad,
    thine arrows did abound.

18 Thy thunder's voice was in the heaven,
    and earth below did quake:
the lightnings lightened all the world:
    earth trembled and did shake.
19 The way wherein thy goings are
    doth lie amidst the sea;
thy path is in the waters great:
    unknown thy footsteps be.

20 When thou thy people ledd'st, then thou
    before them went'st ahead;
yea, like a flock by Moses' hand
    and Aaron's they were led.

PSALM 78

Maschil of Asaph

Tallis

1 GIVE ear, ye that my people are,
    and to my law take heed:
incline your ears unto the words
    that from my mouth proceed.

2 I to you in a parable
    my mouth will open wide,
and utter will the sayings dark
    that from of old abide:

3 Which sayings we have heard and known,
    and us our fathers told.
4 Them from their children we'll not hide,
    but shall the same unfold:
To show the age that is to come
    the praises of the LORD,
his strength and works of wonder done,
    that they might them record.

5 For he a testimony gave
    in Jacob for to stand,
and he in Isr'el made a law
    our fathers to command;
That they unto their children all
    should make them to be known:
6 so that the age which is to come
    might also them be shown;

155

Yea, e'en the children to be born,
    who should arise in turn,
and to their children them declare,
    that so they might them learn:

7 That they might set their hope in God,
    and suffer not to fall
God's works out of their mind, but still
    keep his commandments all:

8 And might not as their fathers be,
    which stubborn were of will,
a generation that rebelled,
    a race perverse and ill;
A generation were they that
    set not their heart aright;
whose spirit was not sound with God,
    nor steadfast in his sight.

9 Lo, Ephraim's children, being armed,
    and bearing with them bows,
did in the day the battle raged
    turn backwards from their foes.

10 God's cov'nant they kept not: to walk
    refused they in his law;

11 his works forgat, his wonders which
    he had them shown before.

12 Things marvellous he also did
    within their fathers' sight;
in Egypt's land and Zoan's field,
    their en'mies to requite.

13 The sea he did divide, and them
    to pass made through the deep;
and there he made the waters stand
    together as an heap.

14 In day-time also with a cloud
    he made them to proceed,
and with a light of fire by night
    he did them onward lead.
15 And in the wilderness the rocks
    he clave and 'sunder rent,
and as out of great depths to them
    gave drink as on they went.

16 He also forth out of the rock
    brought streams of water clear,
and caused the waters running down
    like rivers to appear.
17 And they against him even more
    their sins did multiply,
provoking in the wilderness
    him that is the most High.

18 And God they tempted in their heart,
    meat asking for their lust.
19 Yea, and against God they did speak
    with ill words and unjust;
A table in the wilderness
    can God supply? said they.
20 Behold, he smote the rock, that forth
    the waters gushed straightway;

The streams did overflow: can he
    not also give us bread?
and can he not provide with flesh
    his people whom he'd led?
21 The LORD heard therefore, and was wroth:
    and kindled was a fire
'gainst Jacob; and 'gainst Israel
    there also came up ire;

22 Because in God believed they not,
  nor faith in him would own;
 in that salvation wrought by him
  they trusted not alone:
23 Although the clouds from high above
  commanded forth had he,
 and had the doors of heaven high
  wide open made to be,

24 And manna down on them had rained,
  to feed that multitude:
 and heaven's corn had given them:
25 man did eat angels' food:
 Yea, meat he sent them to the full.
26 In heaven he did make
 an east wind blow: and by his power
  the south wind did awake.

27 Upon them also flesh he rained
  as dust that multiplies,
 and feathered fowls like as the sand
  that on the sea-shore lies:
28 And in the midst of their own camp
  let it descend did he;
 and round about each dwelling-place
  it fell abundantly.

29 So they did eat, and were well filled,
  as they did him require:
 for since it was their will, to them
  he gave their own desire:
30 They were for all this not estranged
  from their own lust, for shame:
 but while their meat was in their mouths,
31 God's wrath upon them came:

158

His anger did upon them fall
    and there the fattest slew;
the chosen men of Israel
    he smote and overthrew.

32 And yet for all this sinned they still,
    and neither did believe
for all his wondrous works, nor would
    their witness once receive.

33 Therefore their days in vanity
    consume did he and waste,
and hence their years in trouble sore
    away did swiftly haste.

34 But when he slew them, then they did
    to seek him show desire:
and they returned, and after God
    right early did inquire.

35 And that God was their rock they did
    to their remembrance call,
and that the high God had for them
    redemption wrought withal.

36 But yet to him they with their mouth
    in flattery drew nigh,
and with their tongues deceitfully
    they unto him did lie.

37 Because that inwardly in heart
    they were with him not right,
and neither in his covenant
    were steadfast in his sight.

38 But, being of compassion full,
    his anger he forgot;
he their iniquity forgave,
    and he destroyed them not:

Yea, many was the time that he
   his anger turned away,
and did not stir up all his ire,
   nor to his wrath gave way.
39 For he remembered that they were
   but frail of flesh and vain;
a wind that passeth soon away,
   and cometh not again.

40 How often in the wilderness
   did they provoke him sore,
and in the desert by their ways
   did grieve him more and more!
41 Yea, they upon him turned their back,
   and tempted God again;
the Holy One of Isr'el they
   with limits did restrain.

42 For they remembered not his hand,
   nor would the day recall,
when from the mighty enemy
   he them delivered all:
43 How he had wrought in Egypt signs,
   the works of his own hand,
and in the field of Zoan shown
   his wonders in the land:

44 And how he had their rivers turned
   to blood from water pure;
their floods the same, that they to drink
   no longer could endure.
45 And divers sorts of flies in swarms
   he did among them send
which them devoured; and noisome frogs
   which of them made an end.

46 Unto the caterpillar he
    gave also their increase,
their labour to the locust-swarms
    which caused their fruit to cease.
47 With hail he did destroy their vines,
    which beaten down were found;
their trees of sycamore with frost
    he withered to the ground.

48 He also gave their cattle up
    unto the fearsome hail,
their flocks to heated thunderbolts,
    which 'gainst them did prevail.
49 His anger's fierceness cast he down
    upon them, forth there went
wrath, indignation, trouble too,
    by evil angels sent.

50 To anger made he way, their soul
    spared not from death to save;
but over to the pestilence
    in wrath their life he gave;
51 And Egypt's first-born all he smote,
    and filled the land with grief;
for in Ham's tabernacles fell
    of all their strength the chief:

52 But his own people like to sheep
    to go forth he did make,
and safely through the wilderness
    them like a flock did take.
53 In safety, so that they feared not,
    them onward lead did he:
but overwhelmed their en'mies were,
    and covered by the sea.

54 He brought them to the border round
    his sanctuary at length;
e'en to this mount, which his right hand
    had purchased by its strength.
55 He also drave the nations out,
    so that they fled apace;
he cast the heathen from the land
    before his people's face.

And for them an inheritance
    by line he did divide:
and made the tribes of Israel
    within their tents abide.
56 And yet they tempted and provoked
    the most high God once more;
and neither steadfastly did keep
    his testimonies sure:

57 But turned unfaithfully, and did
    their fathers' works repeat:
they turned aside were, like a bow
    that worketh with deceit.
58 To wrath they with their places high
    provoked him grievously,
and with their graven images
    him moved to jealousy.

59 When God heard this, then he was moved
    to indignation sore,
and all the house of Israel
    he greatly did abhor:
60 So that the tabernacle he
    of Shiloh did forsake;
the tent which he among men placed
    he desolate did make;

61 And he delivered up his strength
  into captivity,
 his glory even to the hand
  of their strong enemy.
62 His people also gave he up
  unto the sword's sharp edge;
 and he was wroth exceedingly
  with his own heritage.

63 The fire their young men did consume,
  the flames them took away;
 nor given were their maidens fair
  to marriage in their day.
64 Their priests fell by the sword besides,
  and in the grave were laid;
 and yet their widows that were left
  no lamentation made.

65 The Lord awaked as one refreshed,
  that did in sleep recline;
 and like a mighty man that shouts
  by reason of much wine.
66 And straightway in the hinder parts
  he did his en'mies smite,
 and with reproach perpetual
  did throughly them requite.

67 He Joseph's tabernacle famed
  moreover did refuse;
 the favoured tribe of Ephraim
  he neither yet would choose:
68 But chosen out was Judah's tribe,
  he made that tribe rejoice,
 the mount of Zion which he loved:
  mount Zion was his choice.

69 And he his sanctuary built
    like palaces for height,
and like the earth for ever which
    he stablished by his might.

70 He also David chose, that he
    his servant might him make;
and from the sheep-folds, 'midst the sheep,
    him for himself did take:

71 Ewes great with young from following,
    he brought him forth to feed
his people Jacob, Isr'el's house,
    his heritage indeed.

72 According to integrity
    of heart he fed them still;
and by his understanding hands
    he guided them with skill.

PSALM 79

A Psalm of Asaph

Barrow

1 O GOD, into thy heritage
    the heathen way have made;
thy holy temple they've defiled;
    on heaps Jerus'lem laid.

2 The bodies of thy servants dead
    they've given to be meat
to heaven's fowls, and thy saints' flesh
    to beasts of earth to eat.

3 Their blood about Jerusalem
    like water they have shed;
and there was none that bury would
    the bodies of the dead.

4 Unto our neighbours a reproach
    for shame become are we,
scorned and derided by all them
    that round about us be.

5 How long, LORD? is it ever that
    thou shalt deal angrily?
and that like to a flame of fire
    shall burn thy jealousy?
6 On heathen that have known thee not
    thy wrath do thou outpour,
upon the kingdoms on thy name
    that called not heretofore.

7 For Jacob they've devoured, and him
    to be despoiled have made;
and altogether in a waste
    his dwelling-place have laid.
8 To thy remembrance bring no more,
    of thee we humbly pray,
against us our iniquities
    done in a former day.

But let thy tender mercies yet
    prevent us speedily:
because in our affliction sore
    brought very low are we.
9 O God of our salvation, help:
    to thy name glory take:
us free, and purge away our sins,
    e'en for thine own name's sake.

10 O wherefore should the heathen say,
    Where is their God now gone?
Let him be 'mong the heathen known,
    and in our sight each one,

By the revenging of the blood
　　of thine own servants shed,
that thou may'st pay the vengeance due
　　to recompense our dead.

11　Let now the pris'ner's mournful sighs
　　　before thee come on high;
　　by thy great pow'r preserve thou those
　　　that are marked out to die.
12　And let our neighbours sevenfold
　　　paid in their bosom be,
　　with that reproach, O Lord, wherewith
　　　they gave reproach to thee.

13　So we thine own, thy pasture's sheep,
　　　will give thee thanks always:
　　and unto generations all
　　　we will show forth thy praise.

Psalm 80

To the chief Musician upon Shoshannim-Eduth,
A Psalm of Asaph.

Morven

1　HEAR, Isr'el's Shepherd, like a flock
　　　thou that dost Joseph lead;
　　thou that between the cherubims
　　　dost dwell, shine forth indeed.
2　Before Ephraim and Benjamin,
　　　and in Manasseh's sight,
　　do thou arise, stir up thy strength,
　　　come, save us in thy might.

3　Turn us again, O God, we pray,
　　　turn us again to thee;

cause thou thy face on us to shine,
 and so we saved shall be.
4 O thou LORD God of hosts, how long
 wilt thou thine anger show
against the prayer thy people make?
 how long shall it be so?

5 Thou feedest them with their own tears
 which thou dost give for bread,
and mak'st them drink in measure great
 the tears which they have shed.
6 Unto our neighbours us a strife
 thou makest to become:
among themselves our en'mies laugh
 to see us overcome.

7 Turn us again, O God of hosts,
 turn us again to thee;
cause thou thy face on us to shine,
 and so we saved shall be.
8 Thou hast unto thyself brought out
 from Egypt's land a vine;
and thou hast cast the heathen out,
 and planted it as thine.

9 Thou didst prepare before it room,
 that it might there expand;
thou didst it cause to take deep root,
 and so it filled the land.
10 The shadow of it round about
 upon the hills did fall;
and e'en the boughs thereof were like
 the goodly cedars tall.

11 She sent her boughs out to the sea,
    her branches spread abroad:
yea, to the river forth they went:
    thou didst them room afford.
12 Why hast thou therefore broken down
    her hedges everywhere,
that all those which pass by the way
    do pluck her branches there?

13 The boar that comes out of the wood
    doth shamefully it waste,
the wild beast of the field withal
    devoureth it in haste.
14 O God of hosts, we thee beseech,
    return, thine eyes incline;
look down from heaven, and behold,
    and visit thou this vine;

15 And this the vineyard thou didst plant
    by thy right hand alone,
the branch thou strong mad'st for thyself,
    the branch that is thine own.
16 Behold, for it is burned with fire,
    'tis also quite cut down;
thy countenance rebuketh them:
    they perish at thy frown.

17 Let now thine hand be laid upon
    the man of thy right hand,
the son of man whom for thyself
    thou madest strong to stand.
18 So will we not go back from thee,
    nor yet depart at all:
O do thou quicken us, and we
    upon thy name will call.

19 Turn, O Lord God of hosts, again;
    turn us again to thee;
cause thou thy face on us to shine,
    and so we saved shall be.

PSALM 81

To the chief Musician upon Gittith,
A Psalm of Asaph.

Old 81st

1 ALOUD sing unto God our strength,
      with songs do ye rejoice,
and to the God of Jacob make
    a glad and joyful noise.
2 Take ye a psalm, and hither come,
    the timbrel likewise bring,
the pleasant harp and psaltery,
    that ye therewith may sing.

3 Blow up the trumpet at what time
    the moon appeareth new,
in time appointed, on the day
    our solemn feast is due.
4 A statute this for Isr'el was,
    of Jacob's God a law.
5 For this in Joseph he ordained
    a testimony sure;

When he through Egypt's land went out:
    where I a speech did hear,
a language strange, not understood,
    and foreign to my ear.
6 His back I from the burden took,
    his hands from pots did free.
7 Thou didst in trouble on me call,
    and I delivered thee;

169

In secret place of thunder I
    to thee did answer make:
at water-springs of Meribah
    I proof of thee did take.

8 Hear, O my people, and I will
    unto thee testify:
O Isr'el, if thou hearken wilt
    when speak to thee do I:

9 There shall no strange god be in thee;
    and neither yet shalt thou
to any strange god worship give,
    nor down to idols bow.

10 I am the LORD thy God, which thee
    brought out of Egypt's land:
O open wide thy mouth, and I
    will fill it from mine hand.

11 Yet me my people would not hear,
    my voice they would not know;
and Isr'el would have none of me,
    but would a-whoring go.

12 So them I gave up, and them left
    to their hearts' lust alone:
and they from henceforth duly walked
    in counsels of their own.

13 Oh that my people unto me
    had hearkened in those days:
that Isr'el had attentive been
    and walked in all my ways!

14 Their enemies I'd soon subdued
    and driven from their coasts;
my hand I should have turned against
    their adversaries' hosts.

15 The haters of the LORD to him
  ˙had in submission cried:
  but those, their time should have endured,
    for ever to abide.
16 For with the finest of the wheat
    them also fed had he:
  with honey from the rock I'd caused
    thee satisfied to be.

PSALM 82

A Psalm of Asaph

Drumclog

1 GOD in the congregation stands
    of those that mighty be;
  and he among the gods each one
    doth judge with equity.
2 How long will ye unjustly judge,
    perverting judgment right;
  how long accept the persons that
    in wickedness delight?

3 Defend the poor and fatherless,
    and for the helpless plead;
  do justice unto all that are
    afflicted and in need.
4 The poor and needy from their bonds
    deliver and set free;
  them also rid out of the hand
    of those that wicked be.

5 They know not, nor will understand:
    in darkness walk they on;
  lo, all of earth's foundations deep
    out of their course are gone.

6 I have said, Ye are gods; and of
    the most High children all.
7 But ye shall die like men, and like
    one of the princes fall.

8 Arise, O God, stir up thyself,
    the earth to judgment call:
for thou shalt have as heritage
    the heathen nations all.

PSALM 83

A Song or Psalm of Asaph

S. *Magnus*

1 O GOD, no longer silent be,
    from slumber do thou cease:
be thou no longer still, O God,
    and no more hold thy peace.
2 For, lo, thine enemies arise,
    and do a tumult spread:
and they that hatred bear to thee
    have lifted up the head.

3 They counsel taken have against
    the people of thy choice,
and have against thy hidden ones
    consulted with one voice.
4 Said they, Come, let us cut them off;
    let not this nation be:
that from remembrance Isr'el's name
    may perish utterly.

5 Together they consulted have,
    and joined with one consent:
against thee they're confederate,
    agreed without dissent:

6 With Edom's tabernacles join
    those of the Ishmaelites:
of Moab and the Hagarenes;
7   Gebal, the Ammonites,

And Amalek; the Philistines,
    inhabitants of Tyre;
8 yea, Assur's also joined with them:
    together they conspire:
And they Lot's children holpen have.
9   Do unto them each one
as thou didst to the Midianites,
    as was to Sis'ra done,

As unto Jabin, at the brook
    which is at Kison found:
10 which perished at En-dor: as dung
    became they for the ground.
11 Like Oreb and like Zeeb cause thou
    their noblemen to fall:
as Zebah and Zalmunna make
    their mighty princes all:

12 Who said, Let us unto ourselves
    God's habitations take,
that we the same may occupy
    and our possession make.
13 Them, O my God, make like a wheel;
    and as the stubble dry
which driven is about, and tossed,
    before the wind to fly.

14 And as the fire doth burn a wood,
    and as the raging flame

doth set the mountains all ablaze,
    do unto them the same;
15 Them with thy tempest persecute
    that they might be dismayed;
and with the fury of thy storm
    make them to be afraid.

16 Them to confusion bring, and fill
    their faces full of shame;
that they in their perplexity,
    O LORD, may seek thy name.
17 Let them confounded ever be,
    and always troubled sore;
yea, let them all be put to shame,
    and perish evermore:

18 That men may know that thou, whose name
    JEHOVAH is alone,
art over all the earth most high,
    in majesty made known.

PSALM 84

To the chief Musician upon Gittith,
A Psalm for the sons of Korah.

Arnold

1 O THOU that art the LORD of hosts,
    how lovely unto me,
and altogether amiable,
    thy tabernacles be!
2 My soul doth long, yea, faint to find
    the courtyards of the LORD:
my very heart and flesh cry out
    for thee, the living God.

3 Behold, the sparrow findeth out
    an house wherein to rest,
the swallow also for herself
    discovered hath a nest;
Wherein in safety lay her young
    and nourish them may she,
O LORD of hosts, my King and God,
    e'en where thine altars be.

4 Bless'd are they in thy house that dwell,
    they still shall give thee praise.
5 Bless'd is the man whose strength's in thee;
    in whose heart are their ways:
6 Who passing through the valley deep
    of Baca, weeping still,
make it a well: the rain that falls
    the pools doth also fill.

7 They onward go from strength to strength,
    they do unwearied run:
in Zion yet before our God
    appeareth every one.
8 LORD God of hosts, my prayer attend;
    hear, Jacob's God, my plea.
9 Of thine anointed, God our shield,
    the face behold and see.

10 For it is better in thy courts
    but one day to abide,
than elsewhere stay, though it were by
    a thousand multiplied.
I'd rather keep a door within
    the house that's of my God,
than in the tents of wickedness
    to settle mine abode.

11 Because the LORD God unto us
    is both a sun and shield:
the LORD is he that plenteously
    will grace and glory yield.
From them that do uprightly walk
    no good withhold will he:
12 O LORD of hosts, bless'd is the man
    that puts his trust in thee.

PSALM 85

To the chief Musician,
A Psalm for the sons of Korah.

Caithness

1 LORD, thou art he that favourable
    hast been unto thy land:
thou'st Jacob's long captivity
    brought back with mighty hand.
2 Thy people thou forgiven hast
    all their iniquity;
and all the sin which they have done
    hath covered been by thee.

3 Thou taken hast thy wrath away
    which in thine ire had burned:
and from thine anger's fierceness thou
    thyself hast also turned.
4 O turn us, thou that art the God
    of our salvation great,
and do thou cause thine anger strong
    toward us to abate.

5 O wilt thou with us angry be
    for ever past recall?
and wilt thou draw thine anger out
    to generations all?

6 Wilt thou not us revive again
    that quickened we might be,
and that thy people may rejoice
    exceedingly in thee?

7 Thy tender mercy from of old,
    O Lord, unto us show;
and thy salvation bountiful
    do thou on us bestow.
8 I'll God the Lord's speech hear: for peace
    he'll to his own express,
and to his saints: but let them not
    return to foolishness.

9 For his salvation's surely nigh
    to them that do him fear:
that glory in our land may dwell,
    and unto us appear.
10 Because with mercy truth is met,
    together they are found;
both righteousness and peace have kissed,
    as to each other bound.

11 Truth shall out of the earth spring forth
    her bounty to bestow,
and righteousness from heaven high
    shall look on earth below.
12 Yea, what is good the Lord shall give,
    and bring abundant peace;
and so our land in fruitfulness
    shall yield her rich increase.

13 In all his goings righteousness
    before him shall proceed,
and shall us in the pathway set
    wherein his footsteps lead.

PSALM 86

A Prayer of David

Wigtown

1 DO thou bow down thine ear, O LORD,
  and hearken unto me:
because through poverty I am
  in need continually.

2 My soul let be preserved by thee;
  for holy still am I:
O thou my God, thy servant save,
  whose trust in thee doth lie.

3 Since, Lord, I cry to thee each day,
  be merciful to me:

4 rejoice thy servant's soul, for, Lord,
  I lift my soul to thee.

5 For, Lord, thou'rt good, and to forgive
  thou ever art inclined;
and unto all that on thee call
  in mercy rich and kind.

6 Give ear unto the prayer, O LORD,
  which I to thee do send;
and to my supplications' voice
  with speed do thou attend.

7 And in the day I troubled am
  upon thee call I will:
for thou wilt answer give to me
  and my request fulfil.

8 Among the gods there is not one,
  O Lord, like unto thee;
nor are there any works which may
  to thy works likened be.

178

9 All nations whom thou'st made shall come
    and shall thy pow'r acclaim:
before thee they shall worship, Lord,
    and glorify thy name.

10 For thou art great, and by thy hand
    things wonderful are done;
thy greatness all thy works declare,
    for thou art God alone.

11 Teach me thy way, and in thy truth,
    O LORD, my walk shall be:
unite my heart, that I thy name
    may fear continually.

12 O Lord my God, with all my heart
    give praise to thee will I:
and I with joy for evermore
    thy name will glorify.

13 For unto me thy mercy kind
    in greatness doth excel;
and thou delivered hast my soul
    out of the lowest hell.

14 O God, the proud against me rise;
    in their assemblies met
the violent sought my soul, and thee
    before them have not set.

15 But thou, O Lord, a God thou art
    of great compassion full,
of grace, long-suff'ring, mercy kind,
    and truth most plentiful.

16 O turn to me, and mercy have;
    alas, I am undone:
thy strength unto thy servant give,
    and save thine handmaid's son.

17 A token show for good; that they
    which hate me may it see
  and be ashamed: because thou, LORD,
    didst help and comfort me.

PSALM 87

A Psalm or Song for the sons of Korah

Argyle

1 SET in the holy mountains high
    is his foundation sure.
2 Than Jacob's dwellings all the LORD
    doth Zion's gates love more.
3 O city of our God, they speak
    things glorious of thee.
4 Rahab and Babel I'll recall
    to them that know of me:

  Behold Philistia, and Tyre,
    the nations which adorn;
  with distant Ethiopia:
    for there this man was born.
5 But it of Zion shall be said,
    This man, and that man there,
  was born therein: the highest shall
    himself establish her.

6 When he writes up the people, then
    this birth the LORD shall count,
  that this man there was born: he'll write
    the birth from Zion's mount.
7 As well the chosen singers as
    the players there shall be
  on instruments that play with skill:
    my springs are all in thee!

PSALM 88

A Song or Psalm for the sons of Korah, to the chief Musician upon Mahalath Leannoth, Maschil of Heman the Ezrahite.

Dalehurst

1 LORD God of my salvation, hear:
    before thee cried have I
2 both day and night: O let my prayer
    before thee come on high:
Unto my cry incline thine ear:
3   for full of troubles sore
my soul is found, yea, and my life
    nigh to the grave doth draw.

4 I counted am with them that down
    into the pit do go,
and as a man that hath no strength
    am constantly brought low:
5 Free 'mong the dead, like to the slain
    that in the grave do lie,
whom thou recall'st no more: cut off
    as from thy hand to die.

6 Yea, even in the lowest pit
    thou hast me laid and bound,
so that I do in darkness lie,
    and in the deeps am found.
7 On me thy wrath lies hard: thou hast
    made me affliction see
8 with all thy waves: thou'st put far off
    acquaintance mine from me:

As an abomination thou
    hast made them me despise;

I am shut up, and I cannot
    come forth in any wise.
9 By reason of affliction sore
    mine eye doth mourn and cry:
I've daily called, LORD, and to thee
    stretched out my hands have I.

10 Wilt thou show wonders to the dead?
    shall dead rise, praising thee?
11 and shall declared within the grave
    thy loving-kindness be?
Or in destruction, faithfulness?
12   in dark, thy wonders known?
in that land of forgetfulness,
    thy righteousness be shown?

13 But yet I unto thee, O LORD,
    my earnest cry have sent;
and also in the morning-time
    my prayer shall thee prevent.
14 LORD, why is it that thou my soul
    now castest off from thee?
and why is it that thou thy face
    dost hide afar from me?

15 I am afflicted; from my youth
    I ready am to die:
and whilst thy terrors me beset
    distracted sore am I.
16 Thy wrath in fierceness o'er me goes,
    thy terrors make no stay;
17 they've cut me off; they round me came
    like water every day;

Me they together compassed round.
18   Thou hast put far from me
both lover, friend: in darkness thou
  mad'st mine acquaintance be.

PSALM 89

Maschil of Ethan the Ezrahite

Noel

1 I'LL sing the mercies of the LORD
    for ever, and I shall
tell with my mouth thy faithfulness
  to generations all.
2 For I have said, Built up shall be
  thy mercy evermore:
thou'lt stablish in the very heavens
  thy faithfulness most sure.

3 I have a cov'nant made with him
  of whom I have made choice;
to David, that my servant is,
  I sworn have with my voice:
4 That I henceforth for evermore
  thy seed establish shall,
and that I will build up thy throne
  to generations all.

5 The heavens shall thy wonders praise,
  O LORD: thy faithfulness
in congregation of the saints
  they also shall express.
6 For in the heaven who compared
  unto the LORD can be?
who likeness 'mong the mighty's sons
  unto the LORD can see?

183

7 In the assembly of the saints
    God's greatly to be feared;
  and he of all about him is
    to be with awe revered.
8 LORD God of hosts, like unto thee
    who is a strong LORD found?
  or what like to thy faithfulness
    that is about thee round?

9 Thou with thy mighty pow'r dost rule
    the raging of the sea:
  and when the waves thereof arise,
    thou mak'st them still to be.
10 Thou'st Rahab wholly broken up
    in pieces, as one slain;
  with thy strong arm thine enemies
    thou scattered hast amain.

11 The heavens high are thine, the earth
    is also thine alone:
  the world, the fulness all thereof,
    thou'st founded as thine own.
12 The north and south thou by thy strength
    created hast the same:
  lo, Tabor mount and Hermon's heights
    rejoice shall in thy name.

13 Thou hast a mighty arm of old,
    thy pow'r is ever nigh:
  strong is thy hand, its strength is great,
    and thy right hand is high.
14 Justice and judgment of thy throne
    are made the dwelling-place:
  mercy and truth for evermore
    shall go before thy face.

15 Bless'd is the people all that know
  the sound of jubilee:
 in brightness of thy countenance
  their walk, O LORD, shall be.

16 And in thy name shall they rejoice
  with joy throughout the day:
 and greatly in thy righteousness
  exalted be shall they.

17 Because the glory of their strength
  doth only in thee lie:
 and in thy favour shall our horn
  exalted be on high.

18 For our defence the LORD appears,
  and doth us safety bring;
 the Holy One of Israel
  is he that is our king.

19 Then thou didst to thy holy one
  in vision testify,
 and to him saidst, On one laid help
  that mighty is have I;
 One from the people chosen out
  I've made to be renowned,

20 yea, even David, whom I have
  my faithful servant found;

 And with my holy oil have I
21 anointed him: my hand
 with him shall stablished be: mine arm
  shall strengthen him to stand.

22 Upon him there shall not exact
  the mighty enemy;
 nor shall the son of wickedness
  make him affliction see.

23 And I his foes will beat down small
    as dust before his face:
I'll plague them also that him hate,
    and take away their place.
24 But yet my faithfulness to him,
    and mercy, shall be nigh:
and in my holy name his horn
    shall be exalted high.

25 And I will also set his hand
    away out in the sea;
moreover in the rivers far
    there his right hand shall be.
26 Thou art my father, and my God,
    he unto me shall cry,
the rock of my salvation sure,
    that is uplifted high.

27 The first-born also of my choice
    I will him make to be,
and higher than the kings on earth
    exalted be shall he.
28 For him my steadfast mercy keep
    for evermore I will,
the covenant that I have made
    shall stand fast with him still.

29 His seed to come I'll also make
    for ever to endure,
and as the days of heaven shall
    his throne abide secure.
30 If that his children should forsake
    my law and go astray,
and walk not in my judgments just,
    but from them turn away:

31 If also they my statutes break,
  and turn away their heart,
 and do not my commandments keep,
  but from their rule depart:

32 Then their transgression with the rod
  I visit will straightway,
 and their iniquity with stripes
  I surely shall repay.

33 My loving-kindness nonetheless
  quite from him I'll not take,
 nor suffer that my faithfulness
  should wholly him forsake.

34 My cov'nant I'll not break, nor change
  what with my lips said I.

35 Once by my holiness I've sworn,
  I'll not to David lie.

36 His chosen seed assuredly
  endure shall evermore;
 his throne before me as the sun
  shall be established sure.

37 Established also as the moon
  it shall for ever be;
 and as a faithful witness that
  in heaven men shall see.

38 But thou hast cast off and abhorred:
  thine anger forth hath gone;
 thou hast been very wroth with him,
  thine own anointed one.

39 The cov'nant of thy servant poor
  made null and void thou hast:
 thou hast profaned his royal crown,
  and to the ground it cast.

40 Thou'st all his hedges broken down
    and their destruction wrought;
  and thou his strongholds hast destroyed
    and into ruin brought.
41 Each one that passeth by the way
    doth spoil him utterly,
  so that unto his neighbours near
    made a reproach is he.

42 Thou of his adversaries hast
    the right hand set on high;
  and thou'st made all his foes with joy
    themselves to magnify.
43 And thou'st the edge turned of the sword
    held fast within his hand;
  and in the battle that did rage
    thou hast not made him stand.

44 Thou'st made his glory cease, and cast
    his throne down to the ground.
45 His youth thou'st shortened, and with shame
    hast covered him around.
46 How long, Lord? wilt thou hide thyself
    for ever in thine ire?
  how long, is it for ever that
    thy wrath shall burn like fire?

47 Remember thou how short my time,
    how little doth remain:
  O wherefore is it that thou hast
    made all mankind in vain?
48 What man is he of life possessed,
    that death shall never see?
  his soul out of the grave's cruel hand
    deliver up shall he?

49 Thy former loving-kindnesses,
    O Lord, which thou didst swear
to David in thy faithfulness,
    where do they now appear?
50 Mind, Lord, thy servants' ill reproach;
    how in my bosom borne
is of the mighty people all
    the sore reproach and scorn:

51 Wherewith thine en'mies have reproached,
    and, LORD, have mischief done;
wherewith the footsteps they've reproached
    of thine anointed one.
52 For ever blessed be the LORD,
    who doth for aye endure;
Amen, Amen: e'en from this time
    henceforth for evermore.

PSALM 90

A Prayer of Moses the man of God

Dundee

1 LORD, thou hast been our dwelling-place,
    as age to age doth fall,
yea, thou hast been our dwelling-place
    in generations all.
2 Ere mountains forth were brought, or earth
    or world thou'dst formed abroad,
thou e'en from everlasting art
    to everlasting God.

3 Man thou dost to destruction turn,
    and all his works to waste:
and thou dost say, Return, O ye
    men's children: make ye haste;

189

4 Because a thousand years appear
    as no more in thy sight
than yesterday when it is past,
    or than a watch by night.

5 For thou dost carry them away:
    as with a flood they go;
they're as a sleep: they are like grass
    which in the morn doth grow:
6 It flourisheth by morning light,
    and groweth up in strength;
yet in the evening 'tis cut down,
    and withereth at length.

7 For by thine anger 'gainst us shown
    consumed away are we,
and by the kindling of thy wrath
    we greatly troubled be.
8 Before thee our iniquities
    thou settest as unclean;
in brightness of thy countenance
    our secret sins are seen.

9 For all our days are passed away,
    and in thy wrath wax old:
moreover all our years we spend
    just as a tale that's told.
10 Threescore and ten years are the days
    that of our years we see;
and if by reason of more strength
    they fourscore years should be,

Yet is their strength but labour hard,
    and sorrow every day;
for it is soon cut off in death,
    and hence we fly away.

11 For who can ever know the power
    of anger such as thine?
  According even to thy fear,
    so is thy wrath divine.

12 So teach thou us to number well
    our days as they appear,
  that we may thus apply our hearts
    to wisdom in thy fear.

13 Return, O LORD, how long? return,
    let it repent thee yet
  concerning those that do thee serve:
    how long wilt thou forget?

14 O with thy mercy satisfied
    us early cause to be;
  that we may all our days rejoice,
    and so be glad in thee.

15 According to the days wherein
    thou'st us affliction shown
  make thou us glad: e'en as the years
    wherein we've evil known.

16 And to thy servants let thy work
    now in thy pow'r appear,
  and do thou show thy glory forth
    unto their children dear.

17 Moreover let the beauty that
    alone doth appertain
  to him that is the LORD our God
    upon us still remain.

  Of our own hands do thou the work
    upon us stablish sure;
  do thou the work of our own hands
    establish evermore.

PSALM 91

Denfield

1 HE in the secret place that dwells
    of him that is most High,
shall under the Almighty's shade
    abide and safely lie.
2 I therefore of the LORD will say,
    He is my refuge still;
he is my fortress and my God,
    and in him trust I will.

3 He surely shall deliver thee
    and be for thy defence,
both from the fowler's snare and from
    the noisome pestilence.
4 He'll with his feathers cover thee;
    thou shalt thy trust confide
beneath his wings: his truth shall be
    thy shield and buckler tried.

5 Thou shalt not be afraid for all
    the terror of the night;
nor for the arrow that by day
    doth fly while it is light:
6 Nor for the pestilence whose steps
    do in the darkness haste;
nor for destruction openly
    that doth at noonday waste.

7 A thousand at thy side shall fall,
    yea, and ten thousand more
at thy right hand; but unto thee
    it shall not nearer draw.

8 Because that only with thine eyes
    shalt thou behold and see
the just reward that falls upon
    all those that wicked be.

9 Because thou'st made the LORD, which is
    my refuge most secure,
yea, even him that is most High,
    thy habitation sure;
10 There shall no evil thee befall,
    and neither shall it be
that near thy dwelling any plague
    shall come and trouble thee.

11 For over thee he charge shall give
    his angels that him serve,
to keep thee safe in all thy ways,
    that they may thee preserve.
12 They shall together in their hands
    bear up and carry thee,
lest that against a stone thy foot
    dashed in the way should be.

13 The lion thou shalt tread, thy feet
    thou'lt on the adder put:
the lion young and dragon thou
    shalt trample underfoot.
14 Because on me he set his love,
    deliver him will I:
because that he hath known my name,
    I will him set on high.

15 He'll call on me, I'll answer him:
    I will be with him still
in trouble; I'll deliver him,
    and honour him I will.

16 He satisfied shall be when I
    long life on him bestow;
for I to him assuredly
    will my salvation show.

PSALM 92

A Psalm or Song for the sabbath day

S. David

1 TO render thanks unto the LORD
    it is a goodly thing,
and to thy name, O thou most High,
    the praises due to sing:

2 To show thy loving-kindness forth
    when shines the morning light;
and to declare thy faithfulness
    with pleasure every night;

3 Upon a ten-stringed instrument,
    and on the psaltery,
and also on the pleasant harp,
    with solemn sound to thee.

4 For thou, LORD, even through thy work
    hast gladness to me brought:
I triumph will in all the works
    which thine own hands have wrought.

5 How great thy works, O LORD, and deep
    thy thoughts on every hand!
6 A brutish man knows not; a fool
    this doth not understand.
7 What time the wicked spring as grass,
    increasing year by year;
when workers of iniquity
    to flourish do appear;

It is that they shall be destroyed,
   and that for evermore:
8 but thou, LORD, art most high, and thou
   for ever shalt endure.
9 For, lo, thine en'mies, LORD, for, lo,
   thine en'mies perish shall;
the workers of iniquity
   shall hence be scattered all.

10 But like a unicorn my horn
   shalt thou exalt on high:
and newly with the freshest oil
   anointed be shall I.
11 Mine eye shall also my desire
   upon mine en'mies see,
mine ears this of the wicked hear
   that risen 'gainst me be.

12 The righteous like the palm-tree tall
   shall flourish and abound:
he grow shall like a cedar that
   in Lebanon is found.
13 Those in the LORD's house that of him
   most firmly planted be
shall in our God's courts flourish well,
   and yield abundantly.

14 They in old age shall bring forth fruit,
   and shall their strength maintain;
they shall be fat and flourishing,
   their fruit shall still remain;
15 That so they might make manifest
   the LORD's own uprightness:
he is my rock, and there in him
   is no unrighteousness.

PSALM 93

Bangor

1 THE LORD doth reign: with majesty
      he is arrayed and crowned:
   the LORD is clothed with strength, wherewith
      he hath himself girt round:
   The world is also stablished, that
      it cannot once depart.
2 Thy throne is fixed of old, and thou
      from everlasting art.

3 The floods, O LORD, have lifted up;
      they rise with waters swift:
   the floods have lifted up their voice,
      the floods their waves uplift.
4 The LORD on high is more of might
      than many waters' noise,
   yea, than the sea's tumultuous waves,
      and floods that lift the voice.

5 Thy testimonies from of old
      are tried and very sure:
   and holiness thine house becomes,
      O LORD, for evermore.

PSALM 94

Martyrdom

1 O LORD God, unto whom belongs
      the vengeance 'gainst the foe;
   O God, thou unto whom belongs
      the vengeance, thyself show.

2 Lift up thyself, judge of the earth,
      that justice may be done:
   O render thou a due reward
      unto the proud each one.

3 How long, O LORD, shall it be true
      of those that wicked be,
   how long shall it be true that all
      the wicked triumph see?

4 How long shall they give utterance
      and speak hard things and proud?
   and they that work iniquity
      all boast themselves aloud?

5 For they thy people break, O LORD,
      in pieces in their rage;
   and they affliction love to bring
      upon thine heritage.

6 The widow and the sojourner
      despitefully they slay;
   and murder in their cruelty
      the fatherless do they.

7 And yet they say with confidence,
      The LORD this shall not see;
   the God of Jacob neither shall
      regard iniquity.

8 Now understand, ye brutish men,
      that 'mong the people are:
   ye fools, when will ye wisdom learn,
      that be from knowledge far?

9 He that did plant the ear, shall he
      unable be to hear?
   and shall the one that formed the eye
      not see what doth appear?

10 He that the heathen chastens, shall
      he not correctly go?
    and he that knowledge teacheth man,
      shall he the same not know?

11 The LORD doth know that man his thoughts
      from vanity doth draw.

12 Bless'd is the man thou chast'nest, LORD,
      and teachest from thy law;

13 That from days of adversity
      thou rest to him may'st give,
    until the pit be digged for those
      that wickedly do live.

14 Because the LORD will not cast off
      those that his people be,
    and neither his inheritance
      forsake at all will he.

15 But judgment shall return, and shall
      with righteousness unite:
    and all shall follow after it
      that are in heart upright.

16 Who will rise up for me 'gainst those
      that evil-doers be?
    or who will stand for me 'gainst those
      that work iniquity?

17 Unless the LORD had helped, my soul
      in silence almost dwelled.

18 When I said, My foot slips; O LORD,
      thy mercy me upheld.

19 In all the multitude of thoughts
      that do arise in me,
    unto my soul of great delight
      thy kindly comforts be.

20 Shall of iniquity the throne
    have fellowship with thee,
  which frameth mischief by a law
    wrought in iniquity?

21 Against the righteous' soul themselves
    they gather do as one;
  and of the innocent the blood
    they to condemn have gone.

22 But yet the LORD is my defence;
    my God is surely he
  that of my refuge is the rock,
    a stronghold unto me.

23 On them their own iniquity
    he'll bring, and cut them off
  in their own wickedness; them shall
    the LORD our God cut off.

PSALM 95

Winchester

1 O COME, and let us to the LORD
    sing gladly and rejoice,
  and make to our salvation's rock
    a loud and joyful noise.

2 Let us before his presence come
    with thankfulness and praise,
  and with a joyful noise to him
    in psalms our voices raise.

3 The LORD's a great God and great King,
    above all gods he is:

4 earth's places deep are in his hand,
   the strength of hills is his.
5 Behold, the sea is his alone,
   for he the same did make:
the dry land also from his hands
   its form at first did take.

6 O come, and let us worship him,
   let us bow down withal:
and let us kneel before the LORD,
   the maker of us all.
7 For he's our God; the people we
   of his own pasture choice,
and of his hand the sheep. Today,
   if ye will hear his voice:

8 Then harden not your heart, as in
   the provocation sore,
the day of strong temptation in
   the wilderness afore:
9 When once your fathers tempted me,
   me proved, my work perceived.
10 I with this generation long,
   for forty years, was grieved;

And said, It is a people that
   do err within their heart;
and from the knowledge of my ways
   in error they depart;
11 To whom I in my wrath did swear,
   and would not it recall,
that they should neither enter in
   nor know my rest at all.

PSALM 96

S. Matthew

1 O SING a new song to the LORD
 with glad and thankful voice:
unto the LORD sing, all the earth,
 and make a joyful noise.
2 Sing ye with gladness to the LORD,
 and bless his name alway;
and his salvation manifold
 show forth from day to day.

3 Among the heathen near and far
 his glory do declare;
and witness to his wondrous works
 among all people bear.
4 Because the LORD on high is great,
 and greatly praised to be:
and far above all other gods
 much to be feared is he.

5 For of the nations on the earth
 the gods are idols all:
but yet the LORD the heavens high
 did into being call.
6 Before him honour great appears,
 and highest majesty;
lo, strength is found, and beauty shines,
 within his sanctuary.

7 Give to the LORD, ye kindred tongues
 that of the people be;
yea, all the glory and the strength
 unto the LORD give ye.

8 Unto the LORD the glory give
    that to his name is due:
come ye into his courts, and bring
    an offering with you.

9 In beauty wrought of holiness,
    O worship ye the LORD:
let all before his presence fear
    throughout the earth abroad.

10 'Mongst heathen say, The LORD doth reign:
    the world shall stablished be
that it shall not be moved: he'll judge
    the people righteously.

11 O let the heavens high rejoice,
    and glad, let earth resound;
and let the sea roar out her voice,
    the fulness thereof sound.

12 The field let joyful be, and all
    that doth to it pertain:
then of the wood shall all the trees
    sound forth with joy again

13 Before the LORD: for he doth come,
    to judge the earth comes he:
he'll judge the world with righteousness,
    his own with verity.

PSALM 97

Lydia

1 THE LORD doth reign; let all the earth
    with thankfulness rejoice;
with gladness let the multitude
    of isles lift up the voice.

2 Him clouds and darkness compass round:
 and of his throne above
both righteousness and judgment just
 the habitation prove.

3 Before him goes a fire, and burns
 his foes about that be.
4 His lightnings lightened all the world:
 earth trembled it to see.
5 Hills at the presence of the LORD
 like melted wax did flow,
when forth the presence of the Lord
 of all the earth did go.

6 The heavens high above declare
 his righteousness brought nigh;
the people all behold and see
 his glory raised on high.
7 Let all that graven images
 do serve confounded be,
those that of idols boast themselves:
 all gods, him worship ye.

8 This Zion heard, and glad was made;
 and Judah's daughters choice,
because of all thy judgments true,
 O LORD, did much rejoice.
9 For thou, O LORD, art high above
 all those on earth that are:
yea, verily above all gods
 thou art exalted far.

10 Hate evil, ye that love the LORD:
 his saints' souls keepeth he;
them he delivers from the hand
 of those that wicked be.

11 Sown for all those that righteous are
 is an abundant light,
and gladness also for all those
 that are in heart upright.

12 Rejoice, ye righteous, in the LORD:
 and at the memory
of his exceeding holiness
 give joyful thanks do ye.

PSALM 98

A Psalm

Ellacombe

1 O SING a new song to the LORD,
 who marv'llous things hath done:
his right hand and his holy arm
 him victory have won.

2 The LORD's made his salvation known:
 his righteousness hath he
showed openly within the sight
 of those that heathen be.

3 His mercy and his truth recalled
 to Isr'el's house hath been:
and of the earth the ends have all
 our God's salvation seen.

4 A joyful noise make to the LORD,
 let all the earth give voice;
a loud noise make, and sing for joy:
 with praise do ye rejoice.

5 Unto the LORD sing with the harp,
 sing with the harp do ye;
and with the singing of a psalm
 make ye sweet melody.

6 With trumpets and with cornet loud,
   high sounding as ye sing,
   make ye a joyful noise in praise
   before the LORD, the King.

7 The sea let roar with mighty voice,
   and all its fulness sound;
   and let the world give voice, with all
   that doth therein abound.

8 The floods aloud let clap their hands
   with glad and joyful noise:
   and both the great and little hills
   together let rejoice

9 Before the LORD; for he doth come,
   to judge the earth comes he:
   he'll judge the world with righteousness,
   his own with equity.

(repeat verse 1)

PSALM 99

Palestrina

1 THE LORD doth reign: the people all
   let tremble this to see;
   he sits between the cherubims:
   the earth let shaken be.

2 For great in Zion is the LORD,
   and greatly to be praised:
   he high above the people all
   in majesty is raised.

3 Of thy name, great and terrible,
   the praise their mouths let fill
   with solemn sound and thankfulness;
   for it is holy still.

4 The king's strength also judgment loves;
    thou stablish'st equity,
thou judgment giv'st and righteousness
    in Jacob uprightly.

5 Do ye exalt the Lord our God,
    before him bow do ye
low at his footstool worshipping;
    for holy still is he.

6 Moses and Aaron 'mong his priests,
    'mong them did Samuel call
upon his name, upon the Lord:
    and them he answered all.

7 He in the cloudy pillar spake:
    they did to him attend;
they kept his testimonies, yea,
    the ord'nance he did send.

8 Thou answer'dst them, O Lord our God:
    thou wast a God withal
that them forgav'st, but vengeance took
    of their inventions all.

9 Do ye exalt the Lord our God,
    and at his holy hill
do ye him worship; for the Lord
    our God is holy still.

Psalm 100

A Psalm of praise

Effingham

1 MAKE to the Lord a joyful noise,
    all lands, with one accord.
2 Before his presence come with songs,
    with gladness serve the Lord.

3 Know ye the LORD that he is God:
     he hath us made to be,
  not we ourselves; his people choice,
     his pasture's sheep are we.

4 Come ye with thanks into his gates,
     into his courts with praise:
  with thankfulness come unto him,
     and bless his name always.

5 The LORD is good; his mercy lasts,
     and is for ever sure;
  his truth to generations all
     endureth evermore.

PSALM 101

A Psalm of David

Winchester

1 I MERCY will and judgment sing:
     I'll sing, O LORD, to thee:
2 with wisdom in a perfect way
     shall my behaviour be.
  O when is it that thou wilt come
     and unto me draw nigh?
  for with a perfect heart and true
     walk in my house will I.

3 Before mine eyes I will allow
     no wicked thing to be:
  I hate their work that turn aside,
     it shall not cleave to me.
4 He shall depart from me that hath
     a froward heart and ill:
  a person that do'th wickedness
     accept I never will.

207

5 I'll cut him off that slandereth
    his neighbour privily:
him with high looks and pride of heart
    I'll suffer not with me.
6 Upon the faithful of the land
    mine eyes shall be, that they
may dwell with me: he'll serve me that
    walks in a perfect way.

7 He that doth work deceitfully
    shall in my house not dwell:
nor tarry in my sight shall he
    that thinketh lies to tell.
8 I'll early from the land destroy
    all wicked men abhorred:
to cut off wicked doers from
    the city of the LORD.

PSALM 102

A Prayer of the afflicted, when he is overwhelmed, and poureth out his complaint
before the LORD.

S. Kilda

1 ATTEND and hear my prayer, O LORD,
    my cry let come to thee:
2 and in the day I troubled am
    hide not thy face from me.
Incline thou unto me thine ear,
    and hearken when I plead:
and in the day when I shall call
    me answer make with speed.

3 Because my days are quite consumed,
    and pass like smoke away;

my bones are also burned in me,
    and as an hearth are they.
4 My heart is smitten sore within,
    as withered grass and dead;
  so that for grief I quite forget
    or care to eat my bread.

5 By reason of my groaning voice
    my bones cleave to my skin.
6 I am like to a pelican
    the wilderness within:
  And I am also like an owl
    in desert lands unknown.
7 I watch, and as a sparrow am
    upon the roof alone.

8 Mine enemies reproach me sore
    with spite the whole day through;
  and they that are against me mad
    are sworn against me too.
9 For ashes I have eaten up
    as bread in days gone by;
  with weeping mingled I my drink
    with tears that I did cry,

10 Because with indignation thou
    in wrath dost on me frown:
  for thou hast lifted me on high,
    and thou hast cast me down.
11 And like a shadow that declines
    my days away do pass;
  and I am also withered up
    and dried like to the grass.

12 But thou, O LORD, assuredly
    for ever shalt endure;
and unto generations all
    is thy remembrance sure.
13 Thou shalt arise, and mercy thou
    shalt have on Zion yet:
the time to favour her is come,
    the time that once was set.

14 For in the very stones thereof
    thy servants take delight,
and do with favour count her dust
    as precious in their sight.
15 So shall the heathen fear the name
    by which the LORD is known,
and all the kings upon the earth
    thy glory likewise own.

16 When Zion by the LORD himself
    built up again shall be,
then in the glory that is his
    appear to men shall he.
17 He will regard the destitute
    and hearken to their cries:
their prayer he also will receive,
    their prayer he'll not despise.

18 This shall be for the age to come
    both written and assured:
so shall the people which shall be
    created praise the LORD.
19 For from his sanctuary's height
    he hath looked down below;
from heaven did the LORD behold
    earth's places high and low;

20 To hear the pris'ner's groaning voice,
    that doth arise on high;
to loose the captives that by men
    appointed are to die;
21 In Zion to declare aloud
    the name that's of the LORD;
to publish in Jerusalem,
    and sound his praise abroad;

22 What time the people of the land
    together gathered are;
the kingdoms too, to serve the LORD,
    assembled from afar.
23 My strength he weakened in the way;
    my days cut short did he;
24 I said, My God, amidst my days
    let me not taken be:

Through generations all endure
25   thy years: of old thou'st laid
the earth's foundation: and thy hands
    the heavens high have made.
26 They perish shall, but thou'lt abide;
    for thou enduring art:
yea, like a garment they'll wax old,
    and they shall all depart;

Thou as a vesture shalt them change,
    and changed they all shall be:
27 but thou for ever art the same,
    no end thy years shall see.
28 The children of thy servants shall
    continually endure;
before thee shall established be
    their seed for evermore.

PSALM 103

A Psalm of David

Coleshill

1 O DO thou bless the LORD, my soul;
       and all that in me is
   be moved his great and holy name
       to magnify and bless.
2 O do thou bless the LORD, my soul,
       and not forgetful be
   of all the plenteous benefits
       he hath bestowed on thee:

3 Who thee all thine iniquities
       doth pardon and forgive;
   who cureth thy diseases all,
       and health to thee doth give;
4 Who doth redeem thy life, that thou
       should'st not destruction see;
   who thee with loving-kindness crowns
       and tender mercies free;

5 Who with good things thy mouth supplies,
       and satisfies at length,
   so that thy youth is quite renewed
       like to the eagle's strength.
6 The LORD doth justice execute
       for those that are distressed,
   yea, righteousness and judgment just
       for all that are oppressed.

7 He unto Moses did of old
       his ways make to be known;
   and he to Isr'el's children did
       his acts cause to be shown.

8 The LORD is very merciful,
    and gracious too is he;
  yea, slow to anger, plenteous
    in mercy rich and free.

9 He will not always us reprove,
    nor endlessly us chide:
  he neither will his anger keep
    for ever to abide.

10 For with us after our own sins
    he hath not dealt at all;
  nor after our iniquities
    rewarded us withal.

11 For as above the earth in height
    the heaven doth appear,
  so also is his mercy great
    toward them that him fear.

12 As far as east is from the west,
    so far away hath he
  caused our transgressions every one
    from us removed to be.

13 Like as a father pitieth
    his children when they cry,
  the LORD them pities that him fear,
    their needs to satisfy.

14 For he our frame knows, and recalls
    that as the dust are we.

15 Man's days are like the grass: and as
    a field-flower groweth he.

16 For over it the wind doth pass,
    and straightway it is gone;

the place thereof it knows no more
    nor looks again thereon.
17 The mercy of the LORD to all
    that in his fear endure
from everlasting doth abide
    to everlasting sure;

Extended is his righteousness
    to children's children far;
18 to such as of his covenant
    the faithful keepers are;
And likewise unto all of those
    that do remember still
all his commandments to observe,
    and every one fulfil.

19 The LORD his throne hath in the heavens
    prepared and stablished sure;
and over all his kingdom great
    doth rule for evermore.
20 His angels that excel in strength,
    O do ye bless the LORD,
that his commandments do, and hear
    the voice that's of his word.

21 Bless ye the LORD, all ye his hosts;
    ye ministers of his,
that do his pleasure, and fulfil
    what pleasing to him is.
22 O do ye bless the LORD, all ye
    his works that him extol,
in places all of his domain:
    the LORD bless, O my soul.

PSALM 104

S. Stephen

1 MY soul, the LORD bless: LORD my God,
    thou art exceeding great:
thou art with highest honour clothed,
    with majesty and state.

2 With light as with a robe thyself
    who coverest about:
who like unto a curtain drawn
    the heavens stretchest out:

3 Who lays his chambers' beams within
    the waters: who doth make
the clouds his chariot: who his way
    on wings of wind doth take:

4 Who doth his angels spirits make,
    his ministers a flame:

5 who hath the earth's foundations laid,
    ne'er to remove the same.

6 As with a garment, with the deep
    thou coveredst it round:
the waters o'er the mountains stood,
    the floods did much abound.

7 At thy rebuke the waters fled,
    depart with speed did they;
yea, at thy thunder's mighty voice
    they hasted far away.

8 They go up by the mountains high,
    and down by valleys steep
unto the place which thou for them
    hast founded in the deep.

215

9 Thou'st set a bound they may not pass,
       for thou dost them restrain;
   that they to cover o'er the earth
       may never turn again.

10 He to the valleys sends the springs,
       which run 'twixt every hill:
11 they to all beasts of field give drink,
       wild asses take their fill.
12 And by them shall the heaven's fowls
       their habitation make,
   which sing among the branches that
       each for her nest doth take.

13 He watereth the hills: they from
       his chambers are supplied;
   and with the fruit of all thy works
       the earth is satisfied.
14 For cattle makes he grass to grow,
       herb that for man doth serve,
   to bring forth food out of the earth
       that might their life preserve.

15 Wine that makes glad the heart of man,
       and oil he doth impart
   to make his face to shine, and bread
       which strengtheneth man's heart.
16 Moreover full of sap appear
       those that the LORD's trees be;
   the cedar-trees of Lebanon,
       which planted firm hath he.

17 These are the trees wherein the birds
       aloft their nests do make:
   and in the fir-trees for herself
       the stork her house doth take.

18 The high hills do a refuge safe
    for all wild goats provide;
the rocks a place of safety give
    in which the conies hide.

19 The moon above appointed he
    for seasons that are sure;
the sun doth know his going down,
    for all his ways endure.

20 Thou darkness mak'st, 'tis night, then beasts
    of forest creep abroad.

21 The lions young roar for their prey,
    and seek their meat from God.

22 The sun ariseth, they themselves
    together gather then,
and in their place they lay them down,
    each sleeping in his den.

23 Man goeth forth unto his work,
    his labour to attend,
until the evening onward draws,
    and doth him homeward send.

24 O LORD, how manifold appear
    thy works most wonderful!
them all in wisdom thou hast made:
    earth's of thy riches full.

25 So doth this great wide sea appear,
    wherein things creeping be,
innum'rable, both small and great,
    yea, all beasts of the sea.

26 There go the ships: leviathan
    thou'st made therein to play.

27 These wait on thee, in season due
    that meat receive they may.

28 That which thou givest unto them
  they gather for their food:
 for thou dost open wide thine hand,
  and they are filled with good.

29 Then thou from them dost hide thy face,
  and they are troubled sore:
 thou tak'st their breath, they die, to dust
  they turn to live no more.

30 When thou dost send thy spirit forth,
  then they created are:
 behold, thou dost renew again
  earth's face both near and far.

31 Unto all ages shall endure
  the glory of the LORD;
 and greatly shall the LORD rejoice
  in all his works abroad.

32 When he upon the earth doth look,
  it trembleth in its fear:
 and when he doth but touch the hills,
  then they to smoke appear.

33 I gladly to the LORD will sing
  as long as I shall live:
 while I have being to my God
  in songs I praise will give.

34 The meditation of my heart
  shall sweetness me afford:
 of him I'll muse, and truly glad
  I will be in the LORD.

35 From earth let sinners be consumed;
  let not the wicked be.
 O do thou bless the LORD, my soul.
  Praise to the LORD give ye.

PSALM 105

Ellacombe

1 O GIVE ye thanks unto the LORD,
    and call upon his name:
among the people everywhere
    his wondrous deeds proclaim.

2 Sing ye with gladness unto him,
    sing psalms to him each one:
talk ye of all his wondrous works,
    the deeds that he hath done:

3 The glory of his holy name
    advance with one accord:
and let the heart of all of them
    rejoice that seek the LORD.

4 The LORD and his almighty strength
    seek ye continually:
the brightness of his countenance
    for evermore seek ye.

5 Remember ye the marv'llous works
    that by his hand were done;
his wonders, and the judgments that
    forth from his mouth have gone;

6 O ye the seed of Abraham,
    his servant choice indeed,
of Jacob's children the elect,
    the called and chosen seed.

7 To generations all he is
    the LORD our God alone:
his judgments, which most righteous are,
    throughout the earth are known.

219

8　His cov'nant he remembered hath
　　　that it should ever stand,
　　till thousand generations pass,
　　　the word he did command.

9　Which cov'nant, made with Abraham,
　　　his oath, that Isaac saw,
10　he unto Jacob did confirm,
　　　and stablished for a law;
　　An everlasting cov'nant this
11　　to Isr'el: and, saith he,
　　For lot of your inheritance
　　　I'll Canaan's land give thee:

12　When they in number were of men
　　　but few, yea, very few;
　　and in the land were sojourners,
　　　and strangers passing through.
13　When from one nation they unto
　　　another nation went;
　　and from one kingdom they were thence
　　　to other people sent;

14　He suffered none to do them wrong,
　　　no man to do them harm;
　　yea, for their sakes reproved he kings:
　　　the mighty took alarm;
15　For he did say, Touch ye not those
　　　that mine anointed be;
　　nor do those prophets any harm
　　　that chosen are by me.

16　Moreover he a famine called
　　　to come upon the land:
　　so that the whole staff of their bread
　　　he brake within their hand.

17 For he a man before them sent,
    and Joseph was his name,
who into servitude was sold,
    and under bondage came:

18 Whose feet they hurt with fetters cruel,
    in iron they made him lie:
19 until the time that his word came:
    the LORD's word did him try.
20 The king then sent to set him loose,
    and him delivered he;
the people's ruler even sent,
    and him he let go free.

21 And lord he made him of his house,
    that he should be obeyed;
of all his substance ruler he
    throughout the land him made:
22 To bind his princes honourable
    his pleasure to await;
and wisdom teach his senators
    which in the land were great.

23 Moreover into Egypt's land
    the house of Isr'el came;
and Jacob in the land of Ham
    a sojourner became.
24 And there his people much increase
    in multitude did he;
and stronger than their enemies
    he did them make to be.

25 To hate his people he their heart
    did turn at his command,
to deal in subtlety with all
    his servants in their land.

26 His servant Moses he did send,
　　and chosen Aaron too:
27 they 'mong them showed his signs, in Ham
　　his wonders brought to view.

28 He darkness sent, and made it dark;
　　no light did there appear:
　　against his word rebelled they not,
　　for they his wrath did fear.
29 He turned their waters into blood,
　　and he their fish did slay.
30 Abundantly their land bred frogs;
　　kings' chambers entered they.

31 He spake, of flies came divers sorts,
　　and lice in their coasts all.
32 He gave them hail for rain; with flames
　　fire in their land did fall.
33 He also smote their vines and figs,
　　and brake trees of their coasts.
34 He spake, unnumbered locusts came
　　and caterpillar hosts;

35 And they did eat up all the herbs
　　which in their land were found,
　　and did devour of every fruit
　　brought forth out of their ground.
36 And all the first-born in their land
　　in wrath he also smote,
　　the very chief of all their strength,
　　and of their men of note.

37 And he did also bring them forth
　　with silver and with gold:
　　of feeble persons there was none
　　among their tribes of old.

38 When they departed, Egypt then
  was glad that they had gone:
because the fear of them did fall
  upon them every one.

39 And he did spread a cloud for them,
  a cov'ring in their sight;
and fire he gave to lighten them
  in darkness through the night.

40 The people asked, and quails he brought,
  and did them satisfy
with bread which he for them called forth
  from heaven's store on high.

41 The rock he opened in their sight,
  the waters gushed out clear;
in places dry they ran, and like
  a river did appear.

42 Because his holy promise he
  did think upon anew,
and did remember Abraham
  that was his servant true.

43 Moreover he with joy brought forth
  his people whom he'd freed:
his chosen forth with gladness came,
  with songs the promised seed:

44 And of the heathen he to them
  did give the fertile lands:
the labour they inherited
  of heathen people's hands;

45 That they the statutes might observe
  that unto them gave he,
and that they might keep fast his laws.
  Praise to the LORD give ye.

PSALM 106

Dunfermline

1 PRAISE ye the LORD. O to the LORD
    give thanks; for good is he:
for still his mercy doth endure,
    and evermore shall be.
2 Who utter can the mighty acts,
    the deeds wrought of the LORD?
or who can show forth all his praise,
    or tell his works abroad?

3 They blessed are that judgment just
    do constantly preserve;
and also he that righteousness
    at all times doth observe.
4 With favour to thy people borne,
    O LORD, remember me:
to visit me do thou draw near
    with thy salvation free;

5 That I may see thy chosen's good,
    and with thy nation may
in gladness joy, and glory with
    thine heritage for aye.
6 But we have with our fathers sinned,
    and sore iniquity
against thee we committed have,
    we have done wickedly.

7 Our fathers which before us were
    did neither understand
nor grasp the wonders which were wrought
    in Egypt by thy hand;

The multitude of mercies thine
    remembered they no more;
but at the sea, e'en that Red sea,
    wrought provocation sore.

8 But nonetheless he did them save,
    for his name's sake alone,
that he might make his mighty power
    unto them to be known.

9 The Red sea also he rebuked:
    dried up it was straightway;
through depths, as through the wilderness,
    he led them on their way.

10 And save them from the hand of him
    that hated them did he;
and them redeemed out of the hand
    of their strong enemy.

11 The waters covered all their foes,
    and of them left was none.

12 Then they believed the words he spake,
    and sang his praise each one.

13 And yet they soon forgat his works,
    and from his ways they erred;
they for his counsel waited not,
    nor tarried for his word:

14 But they within the wilderness
    did lust exceedingly;
and God they in the desert wastes
    did tempt presumptuously.

15 And he to them gave their request,
    and did their cry attend;
but notwithstanding leanness he
    into their soul did send.

16 'Gainst Moses also in the camp
    to envy they were stirred;
  against the LORD's saint Aaron, too,
    their murmuring was heard.

17 The earth her mouth did open wide
    and swallowed Dathan whole;
  and of Abiram's company
    was covered every soul.

18 And straightway in their company
    there kindled was a fire;
  the raging flame thereof burned up
    the wicked in his ire.

19 The people also at that time
    a calf in Horeb made;
  and to the molten image they
    their homage duly paid.

20 Into the likeness of an ox
    their glory change did they,
  yea, to a beast's similitude
    that eateth grass or hay.

21 So God their saviour they forgat
    and put from mind each one,
  which had in Egypt's land for them
    things great and mighty done;

22 Works wondrous in the land of Ham,
    which unto them appeared;
  things by the Red sea terrible,
    and deeds the people feared.

23 He therefore said he'd them destroy,
    had Moses, choice, not stood
  in breach before him, wrath to turn,
    lest he destroy them should.

24 Yea, they despised the pleasant land,
    and disbelieved his word:
25 and, murm'ring in their tents, would not
    the voice hear of the LORD.

26 Then 'gainst them lifted he his hand,
    and did his anger show,
    that he might in the wilderness
    the people overthrow.
27 Yea, and to overthrow their seed
    among the nations far;
    and them to scatter in the lands
    that strange and distant are.

28 They joined themselves to Baal-peor
    and did their lust fulfil,
    and of the off'rings of the dead
    they freely took their fill.
29 Thus they with their inventions did
    to anger him provoke:
    and with the kindling of his wrath
    the plague upon them broke.

30 Then Phinehas rose in their midst
    and uprightness displayed:
    he judgment just did execute,
    and so the plague was stayed.
31 And that to him for righteousness
    was reckoned as most sure,
    e'en unto generations all
    henceforth for evermore.

32 They also did him anger at
    the water-springs of strife,
    so that it even for their sakes
    went ill with Moses' life:

33 Because his spirit they provoked,
     which holy was and meek,
   so that most unadvisedly
     he with his lips did speak.

34 The nations they did not destroy,
     but suffered them to live,
   concerning whom the LORD to them
     did strict commandment give;
35 They mingled 'mong the heathen were,
     and learned their works for shame,
36 and served their idols; which to them
     a grievous snare became.

37 Yea, they to devils sacrificed
     their sons and daughters fair;
38 they shed the blood of innocents,
     nor would their children spare:
   Their sons' blood, and their daughters' too,
     whom sacrifice did they
   to Canaan's idols: and with blood
     the land polluted lay.

39 Thus they defiled were with the works
     they 'gainst him did invent;
   and likewise they a-whoring with
     their own inventions went.
40 Against his people therefore wrath
     was kindled from the LORD,
   yea, insomuch that he his own
     inheritance abhorred.

41 And them he in his anger gave
     into the heathen's hand;

and they that hatred bare to them
    had over them command.
42 Against them there their enemies
    oppression also wrought;
and underneath their hand were they
    into subjection brought.

43 He many times delivered them;
    but with their counsel he
was much provoked, and them brought low
    for their iniquity.
44 He nonetheless their low estate
    regarded from on high,
and was by their affliction moved,
    when he did hear their cry:

45 For them his cov'nant he recalled,
    which once he did conclude:
and did repent according to
    his mercies' multitude.
46 And to be pitied in distress
    them also make did he
of those that carried them afar
    into captivity.

47 Save, LORD our God; from heathen's midst
    us gather and upraise,
to give thanks to thy holy name,
    and triumph in thy praise.
48 The LORD, the God of Isr'el, blessed
    to everlasting be.
Let all the people say, Amen.
    Praise to the LORD give ye.

PSALM 107

Amazing Grace

1 O GIVE ye thanks unto the LORD,
    for good indeed is he:
for still his mercy doth endure,
    and evermore shall be.
2 Let those that are the LORD's redeemed
    to say so take delight,
whom he out of the en'my's hand
    redeemed hath by his might;

3 And gathered them out of the lands
    that strange and distant be;
yea, call them forth from east and west,
    from north and south did he.
4 They wandered in the wilderness,
    a solitary way;
no city found in which to dwell,
    no place where they might stay.

5 From hunger and from thirst they pined,
    and sighed in their complaint;
yea, in a dry and thirsty land
    their soul in them did faint.
6 'Twas then that to the LORD they cried,
    and did in trouble call:
he heard and he delivered them
    from their distresses all.

7 He by the right way led them forth,
    and them the path did show,
that they unto a city might
    of habitation go.

8 Oh, would that men might praise the LORD
    for all his goodness then,
  and for his works most wonderful
    to children born of men!

9 Because the soul that longing is
    well satisfy doth he;
  and he doth fill the hungry soul
    with goodness rich and free.
10 Such as in darkness sit and mourn,
    beneath death's shadow found;
  who being laid in iron and chains
    are with affliction bound:

11 Because they in rebellion rose
    and did God's words deny,
  and did the counsel wise contemn
    of him that is most High:
12 He therefore did their heart bring down
    with labour hard indeed;
  and down they fell, and there was none
    to help them in their need.

13 'Twas then that to the LORD they cried,
    and did in trouble call:
  he heard them and he did them save
    from their distresses all.
14 From darkness and death's shadow he
    to safety did them take;
  and loosing them each one, their bands
    in sunder he did break.

15 Oh, would that men might praise the LORD
    for all his goodness then,
  and for his works most wonderful
    to children born of men!

16 For quite in pieces broken up
   the gates of brass hath he,
and cut the mighty bars of iron
   in sunder utterly.

17 Because of their transgression fools
   afflicted do become;
and they for their iniquities
   are wholly overcome.
18 Their soul doth with abhorrence view
   all kinds and sorts of meat;
they to the gates of death draw near,
   they can no longer eat.

19 'Tis then that to the LORD they cry,
   and in their trouble call:
he heareth and he doth them save
   from their distresses all.
20 He did his word send forth, and them
   to health he did restore:
he sent, yea, he delivered them
   from their destructions sore.

21 Oh, would that men might praise the LORD
   for all his goodness then,
and for his works most wonderful
   to children born of men!
22 Thanksgiving's sacrifices let
   them sacrifice each one,
and with rejoicing great declare
   the works that he hath done.

23 They that in waters great do trade,
   in ships upon the sea,
24 the LORD's works and his wonders view
   within the deep that be.

25 For he commandeth, and doth raise
  the stormy wind to blow,
which lifteth up the waves thereof,
  and drives them to and fro.

26 They up unto the heaven mount,
  and down they go again
unto the depths: their soul doth melt;
  in trouble they complain.

27 For to and fro, alas, they reel,
  and can no more contend:
they stagger like a drunken man,
  and are at their wits' end.

28 'Tis then that to the LORD they cry,
  and in their trouble call:
he heareth and he bringeth them
  from their distresses all.

29 The angry storm to be a calm
  he maketh at his will,
so that the raging seas subside,
  and all their waves are still.

30 Then are they glad because they're quiet,
  the storm now overpast:
so to the haven they desired
  he bringeth them at last.

31 Oh, would that men might praise the LORD
  for all his goodness then,
and for his works most wonderful
  to children born of men!

32 In people's congregation him
  let them exalt on high;
and the assembled elders let
  him praise and magnify.

33 He turneth to a wilderness
 the rivers that abound,
and likewise all the water-springs
 to dry and dusty ground;

34 A fruitful land he barren makes,
 no more to yield increase,
for all the wickedness of them
 that dwell therein at ease.

35 And he the wilderness doth turn
 to standing water clear;
the dry ground as the water-springs
 he maketh to appear.

36 The hungry also he doth make
 to dwell in plenty there,
that for their habitation they
 a city may prepare;

37 And sow the fields, and vineyards plant,
 about the city round,
which may them fruits of increase yield
 in plenty from the ground.

38 So that they're greatly multiplied
 he doth them bless with peace,
and neither suffers he at all
 their cattle to decrease.

39 Again they minished are with want,
 brought through oppression low;
affliction suffer they afresh,
 and newly sorrow know.

40 On princes he doth pour contempt,
 and causeth them to stray,
to wander in the wilderness
 wherein there is no way.

41 Yet setteth he the poor on high,
    from all affliction free;
and maketh him in families
    just like a flock to be.

42 The just shall see it and be glad,
    rejoicing in the same;
and all iniquity, abashed,
    shall stop her mouth for shame.

43 Whoso is wise, and will observe
    these things sent from his hand,
the loving-kindness of the LORD
    e'en they shall understand.

PSALM 108

A Song or Psalm of David

Noel

1 MY heart is fixed, O God, I'll sing;
    my glory's praise I'll give:
2 wake, psalt'ry, harp: I'll early wake,
    and praise thee while I live.

3 I will thee gladly praise, O LORD,
    among the people still:
among the nations unto thee
    in praises sing I will.

4 For over all the heavens high
    thy mercy's great and free:
and even to the clouds above
    doth reach thy verity.

5 Be thou, O God, exalted far
    above the heavens high:

yea, over all the earth do thou
    thy glory magnify;

6 That thy beloved, whom thou'st loved,
     deliverance may see:
    O do thou save with thy right hand,
     and answer give to me.

7 God spake forth in his holiness:
     Rejoicing I'll prevail,
    Shechem by lot will I divide,
     and mete out Succoth's vale.

8 For Gilead is mine; yea, mine
     Manasseh proves to be;
    Ephraim is of mine head the strength;
     law Judah gives by me;

9 My wash-pot Moab is; I will
     o'er Edom cast my shoe;
    and over thee, Philistia,
     I'll go in triumph too.

10 Who will into the city strong
     me bring with outstretched hand?
    who will me guide upon the way
     that leads to Edom's land?

11 Wilt thou not, O our God, though thou
     hadst cast us off before?
    wilt thou not go forth with our hosts,
     O God, as heretofore?

12 From trouble help us: vain is found
     the help man doth propose.

13 Through God we shall do valiantly:
     he shall tread down our foes.

PSALM 109

To the chief Musician, A Psalm of David.

S. Agnes

1 HOLD not thy peace, God of my praise;
2   the wicked's mouth in pride,
and that of the deceitful man,
    are 'gainst me opened wide:
For they against me spoken have
    e'en with a tongue that lies:
3 they compassed me about, and they
    with words of hatred rise;

They 'gainst me fought without a cause.
4   They for my love and care
mine adversaries are, but I
    will give myself to prayer.
5 They evil have rewarded me,
    and ill for good repaid;
moreover, for my love to them,
    they hatred have displayed.

6 O do thou set up over him
    a wicked man and ill:
let Satan stand at his right hand,
    his adversary still.
7 And when he is to judgment brought,
    condemned then let him be:
sin let his every prayer become,
    shut out unheard by thee.

8 Do thou diminish all his years,
    and let his days be few;
his office let another take.
    These things wilt thou not do?

9 His children let be fatherless,
    his wife a widow lone:
10 his children let continually
    as vagabonds be known;

And let his children always beg:
    and ever seek their bread
out of their places desolate,
    that barren are and dead.
11 And let the hard extortioner
    catch all that he can find;
his labour let the strangers spoil,
    and nothing leave behind.

12 Let there be none that mercy shall
    unto him ever show:
and let his children fatherless
    ne'er any favour know.
13 Let his posterity decay
    the ages all throughout:
let in the generation next
    their name be blotted out.

14 His fathers' past iniquity
    remember let the LORD;
and never let be blotted out
    his mother's sin abhorred:
15 Let them before the LORD be brought,
    appearing constantly;
that he may cut off from the earth
    their very memory.

16 For mercy he remembered not,
    but hunted as his prey
the poor and needy, that he might
    the broken-hearted slay.

17 As he loved cursing, unto him
     so let it now return:
  as he delighted not to bless,
     let blessing from him turn.

18 As garment-like he clothed himself
     with cursing, let it go
  like water in his bowels, like oil
     that in his bones doth flow.

19 And like the garment cov'ring him
     let it unto him be,
  and for a girdle wherewith girt
     continually is he.

20 Let to mine adversaries this
     the LORD's reward be found,
  and to them that against my soul
     in evil speech abound.

21 But do thou for thine own name's sake
     for me, O GOD the Lord;
  because thy mercy's good, to me
     deliverance afford.

22 Because from me my poverty
     and need do not depart,
  and in my trouble wounded sore
     within me is my heart.

23 For I am like the shadow gone
     when it doth fade away:
  I like the locust up and down
     am tossed about alway.

24 My knees are weak through fasting long;
     my flesh of fat doth fail.
25 I to them a reproach became
     that over me prevail:

They looked on me and shook their heads:
26   help, LORD my God, me send:
according to thy mercy great
    O save and me defend:

27 That they may know that from thy hand
    this judgment forth hath gone;
that thou thyself alone, O LORD,
    most surely hast it done.

28 Let them with cursing fill their mouth,
    to bless lift thou thy voice;
when they arise, let them be shamed:
    thy servant let rejoice.

29 Shame let mine adversaries clothe,
    let them themselves gird round
with their confusion great, as with
    a mantle clothed around.

30 And thereupon I with my mouth
    will greatly praise the LORD;
yea, I among the multitude
    will sound his praise abroad.

31 For he shall stand at his right hand
    who is in poverty,
that from those that condemn his soul
    he might delivered be.

PSALM 110

A Psalm of David

Evan

1 THE LORD said to my Lord, Sit thou
    at my right hand on high,
until each of thine enemies
    thy footstool make shall I.

2 The LORD the rod of thine own strength
  shall out of Zion send:
'midst those that are thine enemies
  do thou thy rule extend.

3 Thy people willing in the day
  of thine own pow'r shall be,
in beauties, from the morning's womb,
  of holiness to thee:
Thence hast thou of thy youth the dew.
4 The LORD unto me swore,
and he will not repent, Thou art
  a priest for evermore:

The order of Melchizedek
  thy priesthood is alike.
5 The Lord at thy right hand through kings
  in his wrath's day shall strike.
6 He shall among the heathen judge,
  he'll with the bodies dead
the places fill; o'er many lands
  he wound shall every head.

7 And in the way that he doth take
  drink of the brook shall he:
and therefore also shall the head
  by him uplifted be.

PSALM 111

Newington

1 PRAISE ye the LORD. With my whole heart
  the LORD's praise I'll declare,
where the upright's assembly and
  the congregation are.

2 The works wrought of the LORD are great,
    and do excel in might;
sought out they are of all of them
    that do therein delight.

3 The work he do'th is honourable,
    and glorious besides:
his righteousness established is,
    and evermore abides.
4 He made to be remembered hath
    his works most wonderful:
the LORD is gracious in his ways,
    and of compassion full.

5 Unto all them that do him fear
    their meat hath given he:
and mindful of his covenant
    he evermore will be.
6 The power of his works he hath
    unto his people shown,
that he the heathen's heritage
    may give them as their own.

7 His handiworks are verity,
    and wrought in judgment sound:
all his commandments are most sure,
    and do in truth abound;
8 Stand fast do they with constancy
    for ever to remain;
and, done in truth and uprightness,
    they verity maintain.

9 Unto his people all he sent
    redemption sealed and sure:
commanded he his covenant
    to stand for evermore.

His name is holy, and doth him
    due reverence afford.
10 Of wisdom the beginning is
    the true fear of the LORD.

Good understanding have all they
    that his commandments do:
for ever doth endure the praise
    which unto him is due.

PSALM 112

Gräfenberg

1 PRAISE ye the LORD. Bless'd is the man
    that truly fears the LORD,
to whom all his commandments pure
    do great delight afford.
2 His seed and his posterity
    on earth shall mighty be:
the upright's generation shall
    be greatly bless'd of thee.

3 Both wealth and riches shall be his,
    within his house secure:
and over all his righteousness
    for ever doth endure.
4 Light in the darkness doth arise
    to make the upright see:
he's gracious, of compassion full,
    a righteous man is he.

5 A good man favour doth bestow,
    and is disposed to lend:
he with discretion his affairs
    will guide unto the end.

6 Assuredly he'll not be moved,
   nor ever turned aside:
the righteous in remembrance shall
   for evermore abide.

7 He evil tidings shall not fear,
   nor threatenings from abroad:
his heart is altogether fixed
   and trusting in the LORD.
8 His heart established is and set,
   afraid he shall not be,
until upon his enemies
   he his desire shall see.

9 He to the poor hath gifts dispersed:
   for ever doth abide
his righteousness: with honour shall
   his horn be magnified.
10 The wicked shall it see, and grieve;
   he'll gnash his teeth with ire,
and melt away: for perish shall
   the wicked's chief desire.

PSALM 113

Wiltshire

1 PRAISE ye the LORD. O give ye praise,
   ye servants of the LORD:
unto the LORD's most holy name
   give praise with one accord.
2 O let the LORD's name blessed be,
   which ever doth endure;
yea, even from this present time,
   henceforth for evermore.

3 From rising sun to where it sets
    the LORD's name's to be praised:
4 'bove nations all the LORD is high,
    'bove heav'ns his glory's raised.

5 Who's like the LORD our God, who dwells
6   on high, who humbleth low
himself the things in heav'n to view,
    and in the earth below!

7 Out of the dust he raiseth up
    the poor that fallen be;
out of the dunghill, from the mire,
    the needy lifteth he:
8 That he may him with princes set
    whose rule extends afar,
yea, even with the princes great
    that of his people are.

9 The barren woman house to keep
    he maketh, and to be
a mother of her children glad.
    Praise to the LORD give ye.

PSALM 114

There is a Fountain + refrain

1 WHEN Isr'el out of Egypt went,
    the house of Jacob's seed
from 'midst a people that were found
    of language strange indeed;
2 His sanctuary Judah was,
    and Isr'el his domain.
3 The sea it saw and fled, and back
    was Jordan rolled again.

245

4 The mountains also it beheld,
 and skip did they like rams;
and, unto their foundations moved,
 the little hills like lambs.
5 What ailed thee, O thou sea, that thou
 didst in confusion flee?
thou Jordan, that wast driven back,
 O what did trouble thee?

6 Ye mountains, that like rams did skip,
 what ailed that it was so?
and, all ye little hills, like lambs
 why skipped ye to and fro?
7 Earth, tremble thou at this the power
 and presence of the Lord;
yea, at the presence in the earth
 of Jacob's mighty God;

8 Which turned the hard and barren rock
 to standing water clear,
and made of waters from the flint
 a springing fount appear.

(repeat verse 7)

PSALM 115

Grafton

1 NOT unto us, LORD, not to us,
 but for thy mercy's sake
and for thy truth, unto thy name
 do thou the glory take.
2 O wherefore should the heathen say,
 Where is their God now gone?
3 But our God in the heavens is,
 what pleased him he hath done.

4 Their idols silver are and gold,
   work of men's hands they be.
5 Mouths have they, but they do not speak:
   and eyes, but do not see:
6 Ears have they, but they do not hear:
   they noses have withal,
7 but cannot smell: yea, hands have they,
   yet handle not at all:

   Feet have they, but they do not walk:
   their throat they speak not through.
8 They that them make are like to them,
   and all that trust them too.
9 O Isr'el, trust thou in the LORD:
   their help and shield is he.
10 O Aaron's house, trust in the LORD:
   their help and shield is he.

11 Who fear the LORD, trust in the LORD:
   their help and shield is he.
12 The LORD of us hath mindful been:
   and bless us still will he;
   The house of Isr'el he will bless;
   bless Aaron's house he will.
13 He will all them that fear the LORD,
   both small and great, bless still.

14 You and your children shall the LORD
   increase abundantly.
15 The LORD, which heav'n and earth did make,
   hath made you bless'd to be.
16 The heaven, e'en the heavens high,
   unto the LORD pertain:
   but for men's children to possess
   the earth he did ordain.

17 The dead praise to the LORD give not,
    they cannot speak at all,
and neither any that go down
    and into silence fall.
18 But we the LORD with thankful voice
    will bless with one accord,
from this time forth for evermore.
    O do ye praise the LORD.

PSALM 116

Salzburg

1 I LOVE the LORD, because that he
    hath heard my voice and cry;
yea, to my supplications he
    hath hearkened from on high.
2 Because he hath inclined his ear,
    an answer me to give,
I therefore will upon him call
    as long as I shall live.

3 Of death the sorrows and the snares
    did compass me around:
the pains of hell gat hold on me,
    I grief and sorrow found.
4 Then I upon the LORD's name called,
    and did these words declare:
Deliver thou my soul, O LORD,
    I thee beseech in prayer.

5 I know that gracious is the LORD,
    and righteous, too, is he;
yea, for our God is merciful
    and kind exceedingly.

6 The LORD the simple doth preserve,
  and to them aid doth send:
 I was brought low, and unto me
  his help he did extend.

7 Do thou return unto thy rest,
  there, O my soul, to stay;
 because that bountif'lly the LORD
  hath dealt with thee this day.
8 For thou delivered hast my soul,
  that death I should not see:
 mine eyes from weeping, and my feet
  from falling, thou didst free.

9 I in the land of those that live
  will walk the LORD before.
10 I did believe, I therefore spake:
  I was afflicted sore.
11 I said, when I was in my haste,
  that all men liars be.
12 What shall I render to the LORD
  for all his gifts to me?

13 I'll of salvation take the cup,
  and on the LORD's name call.
14 I'll pay my vows now to the LORD
  before his people all.
15 For in the LORD's sight his saints' death
  most precious doth appear:
16 LORD, truly I thy servant am,
  I am thy servant dear:

 I am thine handmaid's son: thou hast
  set loose my bonds for me.
17 I of thanksgiving offer will
  the sacrifice to thee,

And I with joy will lift my voice
    and on the LORD's name call.
18 I'll pay my vows now to the LORD
    before his people all,

19 Assembled gladly in the courts
    that of the LORD's house be;
amidst thee, O Jerusalem.
    Praise to the LORD give ye.

PSALM 117

Tiverton

1 O GIVE ye praise unto the LORD,
    ye nations all that be:
ye people all upon the earth,
    praise unto him give ye.
2 For great his kindness merciful
    appeareth us toward:
the LORD's truth ever doth endure.
    O do ye praise the LORD.

PSALM 118

Martyrdom

1 O GIVE ye thanks unto the LORD;
    for good indeed is he:
because his mercy doth endure,
    and evermore shall be.
2 Let now the seed of Isr'el say,
    His mercy's ever sure.
3 Let now the house of Aaron say,
    His mercy doth endure.

4 · Let them that fear the Lord now say,
    His mercy doth endure,
  and shall to generations all
    abide for evermore.

5 I with my voice called on the Lord
    when with distress beset:
  the Lord me answer gave, and did
    me in a large place set.

6 The Lord himself is on my side;
    I therefore will not fear:
  for what can man do unto me,
    and where shall he appear?

7 The Lord doth take my part with them
    that helpers are to me:
  upon them therefore that me hate
    I my desire shall see.

8 'Tis better in the Lord to trust,
    than on man to rely;
9 'tis better in the Lord to trust,
    than hope in princes high.

10 Against me there encompassed round
    all nations great and small:
  but in the name that's of the Lord
    I will destroy them all.

11 They compassed me about, yea, they
    about me compassed still:
  but in the name that's of the Lord
    destroy them all I will.

12 They compassed me about like bees;
    as thorns' fire quenched are they:
  for in the name that's of the Lord
    I'll them destroy, I say.

13 Thou'st thrust me sore that I might fall:
    the LORD did give me aid.
14 The LORD my strength is and my song:
    he's my salvation made.
15 The voice of glad rejoicing sounds,
    and of salvation free,
within the tabernacles all
    of those that righteous be:

The LORD's right hand do'th valiantly,
16   the LORD's right hand is high,
the LORD's right hand do'th valiantly,
    and doth him magnify.
17 The LORD's works I'll declare; for, lo,
    I shall not die, but live.
18 The LORD me chastened sore, but o'er
    to death did not me give.

19 To me the gates of righteousness
    set open from on high:
behold, I will go into them,
    and praise the LORD will I:
20 This is the LORD's gate, into which
    the righteous enter will.
21 I will thee praise: for me thou heard'st:
    thou'rt my salvation still.

22 That stone is made head-corner which
    the builders did despise:
23 this is the doing of the LORD,
    and marv'llous in our eyes.
24 This is the day the LORD hath made,
    in it we will rejoice:
we will give thanks therein, and sing,
    and gladly lift the voice.

25 Save now, I thee beseech, O Lord:
 O Lord, beseech I thee,
deliver thou, and unto us
 send now prosperity.
26 On him that in the Lord's name comes
 doth blessing surely rest:
we from the house that's of the Lord
 together have you blessed.

27 God is the Lord, which showed us light:
 the sacrifice bind ye
with cords, yea, even to the horns
 that of the altar be.
28 Assuredly thou art my God,
 and give thee praise will I:
yea, verily thou art my God,
 I will thee magnify.

29 O give ye thanks unto the Lord;
 for good indeed is he:
for still his mercy doth endure,
 and evermore shall be.

Psalm 119

ALEPH

The First Part

Sawley

1 O BLESSED are the undefiled
 and upright in the way,
who in the Lord's most holy law
 do walk and do not stray.
2 O blessed are they that do keep
 his testimonies true,
that with the whole heart earnestly
 do after him pursue.

253

3 They also shun iniquity:
    walk in his ways do they.
4 Thou hast us charged with diligence
    thy precepts to obey.
5 O that my ways directed were
    to keep thy statutes sure!
6 I'll not be shamed when I respect
    all thy commandments pure.

7 I will with uprightness of heart
    thee praise with all my might,
  what time thy righteous judgments all
    I shall have learned aright.
8 Thy statutes I have purposed that
    I keep will, and not break:
  O do not then, I thee beseech,
    me utterly forsake.

BETH

The Second Part

S. Flavian

9 Wherewithal shall a young man cleanse
    and purify his way?
  If he, according to thy word,
    take heed thereto each day.

10 Continually with my whole heart
    I sought have after thee:
  O let me not a wanderer
    from thy commandments be.

11 Thy word I in mine heart have hid,
    lest I against thee sin.
12 Thou blessed art, O LORD: to me
    thy statutes teach within.
13 All thy mouth's judgments to declare
    I have my lips employed.

14 I've in thy testimonies' way
   as in all riches joyed.

15 I'll in thy precepts meditate,
   and all thy ways respect.

16 I'll in thy statutes me delight:
   thy word I'll not neglect.

GIMEL
The Third Part   *Salzburg*

17 Deal with thy servant bountifully,
   and strength to me afford,
   that so I may revive and live,
   and duly keep thy word.

18 O do thou open wide mine eyes,
   I humbly thee implore,
   that wondrous things I may behold
   out of thy holy law.

19 I am a stranger in the earth,
   a sojourner with thee:
   all thy commandments pure disclose,
   and hide them not from me.

20 My soul within me breaketh sore,
   and mourneth day and night,
   for longing that it hath all times
   unto thy judgments right.

21 Thou hast rebuked the haughty proud
   that cursed are each one,
   because from thy commandments pure
   they have in error gone.

22 Reproach, yea, and contempt, I pray,
   remove thou far from me;
   because thy testimonies I
   have kept continually.

23 Against me also there did sit
  and speak the princes great:
  but I thy servant did upon
  thy statutes meditate.

24 The testimonies thou dost give
  are also my delight;
  my counsellors they are besides,
  advising me aright.

DALETH
The Fourth Part

Ballerma

25 My soul unto the dust doth cleave
  in mine affliction sore:
  according to thy word do thou
  me quicken and restore.

26 I have declared my ways each one
  and nothing kept from thee,
  and unto me thou gavest ear:
  thy statutes teach thou me.

27 Make me to understand the way
  of all thy precepts right:
  then of thy works which wondrous are
  I talk shall with delight.

28 My soul doth melt for heaviness,
  and is in me outpoured:
  do thou make haste to strengthen me
  according to thy word.

29 The way of lying take from me;
  grant graciously thy law.

30 Truth's way I've chosen, and have laid
  thy judgments me before.

31 I've to thy testimonies stuck:
  LORD, shame me not, I pray.

32 When thou'lt enlarge my heart, I'll run
    in thy commandments' way.

HE
The Fifth Part
York

33 Do thou, O LORD, unto me teach
    thy statutes' perfect way;
and it unto the end I shall
    keep steadfastly alway.

34 Give understanding unto me,
    and I shall keep thy law;
yea, it with my whole heart I shall
    observe for evermore.

35 Make me to go within the path
    of thy commandments right;
for I therein do pleasure find
    and greatly take delight.

36 Unto thy testimonies sure
    do thou incline my heart,
that it to covetousness may
    from them no more depart.

37 And from beholding vanity
    turn thou mine eyes away;
and do thou me revive again,
    and quicken in thy way.

38 Established to thy servant true
    let thou thy word appear;
and do thou him preserve who is
    devoted to thy fear.

39 Turn my reproach away, for I
    in fear thereof have stood:
for all thy judgments unto me
    both upright are and good.

40 Behold, after thy precepts I
    have longed continually:
O do thou in thy righteousness
    revive and quicken me.

VAV
The Sixth Part

Drumclog

41 Thy tender mercies unto me
    let also come, O LORD,
yea, even thy salvation great,
    according to thy word.
42 So shall I have wherewith I may
    give him an answer just
that me reproacheth wickedly:
    for in thy word I trust.

43 The word of truth out of my mouth
    take thou not utterly;
because I in thy judgments just
    have caused my hope to be.
44 So I thy law continually
    shall keep for evermore.
45 And I will walk at large, because
    I seek thy precepts sure.

46 Before kings unashamed I'll speak
    thy testimonies right.
47 In thy commandments which I've loved
    I will myself delight.
48 To thy commandments which I've loved
    I'll lift my hands on high;
and in thy statutes meditate
    assuredly will I.

258

38

ZAIN
The Seventh Part
Hermon

49 Remember that same word which thou
    didst to thy servant send,
upon the which thou hast me caused
    to hope unto the end.

50 This is the comfort that I do
    in mine affliction see:
for in my sorrow and distress
    thy word hath quickened me.

51 The proud have had me in contempt
    and in derision sore:
yet have I not declined at all
    nor fallen from thy law.

52 The judgments which thou gav'st of old,
    O LORD, remembered I;
and I myself continually
    have comforted thereby.

53 Oh, horror gripped me: for thy law
    the wicked do forsake.

54 I in my house of pilgrimage
    my songs thy statutes make.

55 Thy name I have remembered, LORD,
    by night, and kept thy law.

56 And this I had, because I kept
    thy precepts heretofore.

CHETH
The Eighth Part
Lloyd

57 My portion and inheritance
    art thou, O LORD, alone:
I have resolved and said that I
    would keep thy words each one.

58 With my whole heart thy favour kind
    entreated I of thee:
according to thy word do thou
    be merciful to me.

59 I thought upon my former ways,
    that I each one might try;
and to thy testimonies all
    my feet then turn did I.

60 I hasted, ling'ring not to keep
    all thy commandments pure.

61 Bands of the wicked have me robbed:
    I ne'er forgot thy law.

62 At midnight I to give thee thanks
    will from my bed arise,
because of all thy judgments just
    which are before mine eyes.

63 Companion, I, of all that keep
    thy precepts, fearing thee;

64 O LORD, thy mercy fills the earth:
    thy statutes teach thou me.

TETH
The Ninth Part

Coleshill

65 Well hast thou with thy servant dealt
    in faithfulness, O LORD;
for thou to me hast favour shown
    according to thy word.

66 Do thou good judgment teach, and me
    with knowledge sound endue:
for verily I have believed
    all thy commandments true.

67 Ere I afflicted was I strayed:
    but keep thy word I will.
68 Both good thou art and good thou do'st;
    teach me thy statutes still.
69 Those that are lifted up with pride
    against me forged a lie:
but as for me, with my whole heart
    thy precepts keep will I.

70 Their heart's as fat as grease, but yet
    I in thy law delight.
71 'Tis good I've been afflicted, that
    thy statutes learn I might.
72 For of thy mouth the law to me
    is better and more sure
than many thousands, heaps on heaps,
    of gold and silver pure.

YOD
The Tenth Part   *S. James*

73 Thy hands have made and fashioned me,
    and thou'st me caused to live.
That I may thy commandments learn
    me understanding give.
74 They that thee fear will be right glad
    what time they do me see;
because I in thy holy word
    have hoped continually.

75 That right thy judgments are, O LORD,
    thou hast me caused to know,
and that thou in thy faithfulness
    hast me afflicted so.

76 Thy kindness merciful, I pray,
  let for my comfort be,
according to the word unto
  thy servant sent by thee.

77 O let thy tender mercies come
  to me, that I may live:
because thy just and holy law
  delight to me doth give.

78 The proud let shamed be; for they dealt
  perversely to mine ill
without a cause: but meditate
  I in thy precepts will.

79 Let those with gladness turn to me
  that in thy fear endure,
those also that have known in truth
  thy testimonies sure.

80 My heart let perfect be and sound
  in all thy statutes right;
that I may not be shamed, nor yet
  confounded in thy sight.

CAPH
The Eleventh Part

S. Mary

81 My soul for thy salvation faints:
  hope in thy word I see.

82 Mine eyes fail for thy word: I say,
  When wilt thou comfort me?

83 For like a bottle I'm become
  that in the smoke is set;
but nonetheless thy statutes right
  I never do forget.

84 How many are thy servant's days?
 when wilt thou execute
the judgment due upon all those
 that do me persecute?

85 The haughty proud have digged for me
 deep pits that I might fall,
which after thine own law cannot
 be justified at all.

86 Thy pure commandments every one
 right and most faithful be:
they wrongfully me persecute;
 do thou give help to me.

87 Me they had almost on the earth
 consumed with cruel spite:
but I forsook not, nor did turn
 from all thy precepts right.

88 After thy loving-kindness great
 me quicken and preserve:
the testimony of thy mouth
 so shall I still observe.

LAMED
The Twelfth Part   *London New*

89 Thy word for ever is, O LORD,
 in heaven settled fast.

90 And unto generations all
 thy faithfulness doth last;
The earth thou'st stablished: it abides.

91 Continue they this day
according to thine ord'nances:
 thy servants all are they.

92 Unless that my delights had been
    in thy most holy law,
then had I perished in my grief
    and mine affliction sore.

93 Thy precepts I will ne'er forget:
    with them thou'st quickened me.

94 I'm thine, me save: for I have sought
    thy precepts earnestly.

95 The wicked for me waited have,
    me hoping to destroy:
but yet thy testimonies I
    consider will with joy.

96 Of all perfection I have seen
    an end that is assured:
but thy commandment all excels,
    and is exceeding broad.

MEM
The Thirteenth Part

Stroudwater

97 O how love I thy holy law,
    'tis my delight alway!
it is my meditation sweet,
    my study all the day.

98 Thou hast through thy commandments pure
    me wiser made by far
than all mine enemies, because
    they ever with me are.

99 More understanding I possess
    than all my teachers wise:
for in thy testimonies sure
    my meditation lies.

100 In understanding I excel
    the ancients that are famed;
for by thy precepts, which I keep,
    my conduct I have framed.

101 My feet from each ill way I stayed,
    that I might keep thy word.
102 Since thou'st me taught, I have not from
    thy righteous judgments erred.
103 How sweet thy words are to my taste!
    they sweeter are by far
than choicest honey to my mouth:
    how sweet, how fresh, they are!

104 I through the precepts thou hast taught
    do understanding gain:
and therefore every way that's false
    with hatred I disdain.

NUN
The Fourteenth Part

Caroline

105 Thy word is to my feet a lamp,
    and to my path a light.
106 I sworn have, and I will perform,
    to keep thy judgments right.
107 I am afflicted very much;
    do thou me quicken, Lord:
in all my trouble me revive,
    according to thy word.

108 The free-will off'rings of my mouth
    accept, I thee beseech,
and unto me, O Lord, I pray,
    do thou thy judgments teach.

109 My soul is always in my hand:
  thy law I'll not forget.
110 I from thy precepts erred not, though
  ill men a snare have set.

111 I've taken as an heritage
  thy testimonies sure,
for they my heart's rejoicing are
  henceforth for evermore.
112 I also have inclined my heart,
  and steadfastly intend,
thy statutes alway to perform,
  yea, even to the end.

SAMECH
The Fifteenth Part

Spohr

113 Vain thoughts I hate: but I do love
  thy just and holy law.
114 Thou art my hiding-place and shield:
  hope from thy word I draw.
115 Depart, ye evil-doers all,
  and from me go away:
because my God's commandments I
  will keep with care alway.

116 According to thy holy word
  uphold and strengthen me,
that I may live: and of my hope
  shamed let me never be.
117 Hold thou me up, and so I shall
  be kept in safety still:
and to thy statutes have respect
  continually I will.

118 Thou'st trodden down all them that err
    and from thy statutes stray:
because that with deceitfulness
    in falsehood walk do they.

119 Away like dross thou puttest all
    the wicked of the earth:
thy testimonies I do love
    above all riches' worth.

120 My flesh doth tremble, all dismayed,
    for fear I have of thee;
and I thy righteous judgments all
    do fear exceedingly.

AIN
The Sixteenth Part

Caithness

121 I in thy sight have judgment done,
    and justice also wrought:
to those oppressors leave me not
    that for my hurt have sought.

122 As surety do thou stand for good
    unto thy servant poor:
let not the haughty proud oppress
    nor persecute me sore.

123 My longing eyes do fail, alas,
    for thy salvation great,
and for thy righteousness' pure word,
    which daily I await.

124 According to thy mercy kind
    with thine own servant deal:
and in thy doctrine unto me
    thy statutes right reveal.

125 Because I am thy servant poor,
    me understanding give,
that I thy testimonies true
    may know, and by them live.
126 'Tis time, LORD, that thou work: they have
    made void thy law divine.
127 For thy commandments love I more
    than gold, yea, gold most fine.

128 I therefore firmly do esteem
    thy precepts all, I say,
concerning all things to be right;
    and hate I each false way.

PE
The Seventeenth Part

Evan

129 Thy testimonies from of old
    are wonderful to me:
my soul doth therefore them observe
    and keep with constancy.
130 The entrance of thy words most true
    gives light unto the eyes;
it doth an understanding give
    which makes the simple wise.

131 My mouth in thirst I opened wide
    and panted as one dry:
for after thy commandments all
    long earnestly did I.
132 Upon me look, and merciful
    do thou unto me prove;
as usest thou to do to those
    thy name that truly love.

133 My steps prepare thou in thy word,
  that they might ordered be:
let no iniquity obtain
  dominion over me.

134 Me free from man's oppression cruel:
  thy precepts keep I will.

135 Thy face make on thy servant shine:
  teach me thy statutes still.

136 Rivers of waters from mine eyes
  in mine affliction pour;
because they neither do observe
  nor keep thy holy law.

TZADDI

The Eighteenth Part   *Moravia*

137 LORD, thou art just: upright appear
  the judgments made by thee.

138 Thy testimonies thou command'st
  right and most faithful be.

139 My zeal hath wholly me consumed,
  and doth my strength exceed,
because mine enemies thy words
  forgotten have indeed.

140 Thy word is very pure: on it
  thy servant's love is set.

141 I'm small, despised: yet I do not
  thy precepts once forget.

142 As righteousness eternal doth
  thy righteousness endure;
concerning all thy holy law,
  it is the truth most pure.

143 With trouble anguish hath combined
    and taken hold on me:
  yet my delights amidst my grief
    thy pure commandments be.
144 Thy testimonies' righteousness
    for ever shall remain.
  Give understanding unto me,
    and life I shall obtain.

KOPH
The Nineteenth Part

Kedron

145 With my whole heart I cried, LORD, hear:
    thy statutes keep I will.
146 I cried to thee; me save: I'll keep
    thy testimonies still.
147 I of the morning did prevent
    the dawning, and did cry;
  because each day expectantly
    hope in thy word did I.

148 Mine eyes with wakefulness prevent
    the watches of the night,
  that meditate upon thy word
    with holy zeal I might.
149 Hear thou my voice according to
    thy loving-kindness free:
  according to thy judgment, LORD,
    O do thou quicken me.

150 Who follow mischief they draw nigh:
    they from thy law are far.
151 But thou art near, O LORD; and truth
    all thy commandments are.

152 For as concerning all of those
  thy testimonies pure,
I've known of old thou'st founded them
  for ever to endure.

RESH
The Twentieth Part

Grafton

153 Consider mine affliction great,
  and me in safety set;
deliver thou my soul: for I
  thy law do not forget.

154 Plead thou my cause, and unto me
  deliverance afford:
O quicken and revive thou me
  according to thy word.

155 Salvation's from the wicked far;
  on thee they do not call:
because the statutes thou command'st
  they do not seek at all.

156 Thy tender mercies manifold
  are great, O LORD, and free:
according to thy judgments just
  revive and quicken me.

157 My persecutors and my foes
  against me multiply;
yet from thy testimonies sure
  decline not once do I.

158 When the transgressors I beheld
  which greatly from thee erred,
then was I filled with grief, for they
  kept not thy holy word.

159 Consider how thy precepts all
    I love exceedingly:
  after thy loving-kindness, Lord,
    O do thou quicken me.

160 Thy word from the beginning doth
    abide both true and sure:
  thy righteous judgments every one
    for ever do endure.

SCHIN
The Twenty-first Part

Abney

161 Without a cause have princes great
    me persecuted sore:
  but yet of thy most holy word
    my heart doth stand in awe.

162 I at thy word rejoice, as one
    that on great spoil doth light.

163 Hate and abhor I lying, but
    thy law is my delight.

164 Full seven times a day with joy
    I rise in praise to thee,
  because thy righteous judgments true
    are wonderful to me.

165 Great peace have they which love thy law:
    and them offend shall none.

166 Lord, I've for thy salvation hoped,
    and thy commandments done.

167 My soul thy testimonies hath
    observed most carefully,
  and I moreover each of them
    do love exceedingly.

168 I have thy holy precepts kept
    and testimonies sure:
for of my ways there is not one
    that is not thee before.

TAU
The Twenty-second Part   *S. Columba*

169 O let my earnest voice and cry
    come near before thee, LORD:
give understanding unto me
    according to thy word.

170 O let my supplication come
    before thee, and be heard:
and unto me deliv'rance send
    according to thy word.

171 With gladness shall my lips in praise
    give utterance to thee,
when of thy statutes right thou hast
    the doctrine taught to me.

172 Of thy most holy word my tongue
    shall speak, and it confess:
because all thy commandments true
    are perfect righteousness.

173 Thine hand let give me help; for I
    did choose thy precepts right.

174 I've longed for thy salvation, LORD:
    thy law is my delight.

175 O let my soul revive and live,
    it shall give praise to thee;
and let thy righteous judgments still
    be helpful unto me.

176 I've like a lost sheep gone astray:
  thy servant seek and find;
 for thy commandments I do not
  let slip out of my mind.

PSALM 120

A Song of degrees

Repton

1 UNTO the LORD in my distress
  I cried, and me he heard.
2 From lying lips and guileful tongue
  my soul deliver, LORD.
3 What shall be given thee? or what,
  false tongue, requite thy shame?
4 The mighty's arrows sharp, with coals
  of juniper aflame.

5 Woe is me that, a sojourner,
  I am in Mesech's hand,
 and that I dwell in Kedar's tents,
  a stranger in the land!
6 My soul too long hath dwelt with him
  that peace doth much abhor.
7 I am for peace: but when I speak,
  behold, they are for war.

PSALM 121

A Song of degrees

French

1 I TO the hills will lift mine eyes:
  from whence doth come mine aid?
2 Mine aid comes from the LORD alone,
  which heav'n and earth hath made.

3 He will not suffer from the way
    thy foot removed to be:
he will not into slumber fall
    that safely keepeth thee.

4 Behold, he that keeps Israel
    shall slumber not nor sleep.
5 The LORD thee keeps: the LORD a shade
    on thy right hand doth keep.
6 The sun thee therefore shall not smite,
    nor shall thee harm by day;
the moon by night thee shall not hurt,
    nor cause to thee dismay.

7 From every evil shall the LORD
    preserve and keep thee whole:
he over thee a watch shall keep,
    and shall preserve thy soul.
8 Thy going out and coming in
    the LORD preserveth sure;
from this time forth he shall thee keep,
    and even evermore.

PSALM 122

A Song of degrees of David

Harington

1 I GLAD was when they said to me,
    Let us with one accord
go up into the house that doth
    pertain unto the LORD.
2 Within thy gates, Jerusalem,
    our feet shall standing be.
3 Jerus'lem's as a city built
    together compactly.

4 For thither do the tribes go up,
    the LORD's tribes to the same,
to Isr'el's testimony there,
    to thank the LORD's great name.
5 For thrones of judgment, e'en the thrones
    of David's house, there dwell.
6 Pray for Jerus'lem's peace: they that
    thee love shall prosper well.

7 May peace abide within the walls
    that compass thee around;
and may within thy palaces
    prosperity abound.
8 Now for my brethren, and for all
    that my companions be,
I even for their sakes will say,
    May peace be found in thee.

9 Since of the LORD our God the house
    in thee abideth still,
seek for thy welfare and thy good
    continually I will.

PSALM 123

A Song of degrees

Stracathro

1 O THOU that dwellest in the heavens,
        I lift mine eyes to thee.
2 Behold, as servants' eyes do look
    their masters' hand to see,
And as upon her mistress' hand
    a maiden's eyes attend,
our eyes wait on the LORD our God,
    till he us mercy send.

3 Let mercy on us be, O LORD,
    let mercy on us be:
because that filled with sore contempt
    exceedingly are we.

4 Our soul with scorn of those at ease
    is filled exceedingly,
and with the sore contempt of those
    that proud and lofty be.

PSALM 124

A Song of degrees of David

Brother James' Air

1 HAD not the LORD been on our side,
    may Israel now say;

2 Had not the LORD been on our side,
    when 'gainst us rise did they:

3 When kindled 'gainst us was their wrath,
    they had us swallowed whole:

4 then had the waters us o'erwhelmed,
    the stream gone o'er our soul:

5 Then had the waters proud our soul
    o'erwhelmed and swept away.

6 Bless'd be the LORD, who to their teeth
    us gave not for a prey.

7 Out of the fowlers' snare our soul
    is as a bird set free:
the snare is broken, rent in twain,
    and so escaped are we.

8 Our help and our deliverance
    is in the LORD's great name,
because in him we put our trust
    that heav'n and earth did frame.

Psalm 125

A Song of degrees

S. Kilda

1 THEY in the LORD that put their trust
  as Zion mount shall be,
which cannot be removed, but doth
  abide continually.

2 As round about Jerusalem
  the mountains stand most sure,
the LORD his people compasseth
  henceforth for evermore.

3 The wicked's rod upon the lot
  of just men shall not be,
lest forth the righteous put their hands
  unto iniquity.

4 Do good, O LORD, unto all those
  in goodness that delight,
and also unto them that are
  within their hearts upright.

5 Such as turn to their crooked ways
  the LORD shall lead away
with workers of iniquity:
  on Isr'el peace shall stay.

Psalm 126

A Song of degrees

Caroline

1 WHEN Zion's long captivity
  the LORD turned back again,
then were we likened unto them
  that in a dream remain.

2 Then filled with laughter was our mouth,
      our tongue with song each one:
   they 'mong the heathen said, The LORD
      great things for them hath done.

3 The LORD hath done great things for us,
      as we with joy record.
4 Again turn our captivity,
      as southern streams, O LORD.
5 Who sow in tears shall reap in joy.
6   He that goes forth in pain
   and weepeth, bearing precious seed,
      shall doubtless come again;

   He with rejoicing shall return,
      who sowed with tears the seed;
   yea, bringing back his sheaves with him,
      he shall rejoice indeed.

PSALM 127

A Song of degrees for Solomon

Bishopthorpe

1 EXCEPT the LORD do build the house,
      the builders' labour's vain:
   except the LORD the city keep,
      the watchman wakes in vain.
2 'Tis vain for you to rise betimes;
      to sit, late hours to keep;
   to eat of sorrows' bread: for he
      gives his beloved sleep.

3 Lo, children are an heritage
      that cometh from the LORD:

and of the womb assuredly
   the fruit is his reward.
4 As arrows are within the hand
   of one that is of might,
so are the children of the youth
   grown up and strong to fight.

5 O happy is the man that hath
   his quiver full of these:
they'll unashamed within the gate
   speak with the enemies.

PSALM 128

A Song of degrees

Sawley

1 BLESS'D is each one that fears the LORD;
   that walketh in his ways.
2 For thou the labour of thine hands
   shalt eat throughout thy days:
And happy shalt thou be and blessed;
   it shall be well with thee:
3 and as a fruitful vine thy wife
   by thine house' sides shall be:

Thy children like to olive-plants
   about thy table round.
4 Behold, the man that fears the LORD
   thus blessed shall be found.
5 The LORD shall out of Zion give
   his blessing unto thee:
and of thy life thou all the days
   Jerus'lem's good shalt see.

6 Yea, in thy children's children thou
    shalt see thine own increase;
moreover thou of Isr'el shalt
    behold the settled peace.

PSALM 129

A Song of degrees

Vox Dilecti

1 MANY a time afflicted me
    e'en from my youth have they,
O many, many is the time,
    may Israel now say:
2 Many a time afflicted me
    e'en from my youth have they,
O many times: yet they 'gainst me
    have not prevailed, I say.

3 The ploughers ploughed upon my back:
    they long their furrows drew.
4 The LORD is righteous: he hath cut
    the wicked's cords in two.
5 Confound and turn them back that have
    to Zion hatred shown.
6 As grass on house-tops let them be,
    which withers ere 'tis grown:

7 Wherewith enough to fill his hand
    the mower cannot find;
nor strands to fill his bosom that
    doth labour sheaves to bind.
8 They neither say which do go by,
    The LORD you prosper well;
we in the LORD's name do you bless:
    his blessing on you dwell.

Psalm 130

A Song of degrees

Morven

1 OUT of the depths, Lord, have I cried:
2   Lord, hear my voice to thee;
    let to my supplications' voice
      thine ears attentive be.
3 Lord, who shall stand, Lord, if thou should'st
    observe iniquities?
4 But, so that feared thou mayest be,
    with thee forgiveness is.

5 I for the Lord wait, my soul waits;
    my hope is in his word.
6 More than they that for morning watch,
    my soul waits for the Lord:
    Yea, more than they that watch for morn.
7   Let Israel, I say,
    hope in the Lord: for with the Lord
      is mercy found alway.

    And with him there redemption is,
      both plenteous and free.
8 And from all his iniquities
    Isr'el redeem shall he.

Psalm 131

A Song of degrees of David

Lynton

1 MY heart not haughty is, O Lord,
    mine eyes not lofty be:
    I neither deal in matters great,
      nor things too high for me.

2 I surely have behaved as one
    that quiet is and mild;
for I, as of his mother wean'd,
    am like a little child:

My soul is as a weaned child
    that fretful is no more.
3 Let Israel hope in the LORD
    henceforth for evermore.

PSALM 132

A Song of degrees

Colchester

1 DAVID, and his afflictions all,
    O LORD, remember thou:
2 how to the LORD he sware, and made
    to Jacob's Strength his vow:
3 I surely will not enter in,
    saith he, nor will I tread
the tabernacle of my house,
    nor go up to my bed;

4 I purposed am that I will not
    give sleep unto mine eyes;
nor let mine eyelids slumber take,
    or rest in any wise;
5 Until I do a place find out
    well pleasing to the LORD,
a place that habitation doth
    to Jacob's Strength afford.

6 Lo, from afar we heard thereof:
    at Ephratah it stood;
we did it find amidst the fields
    and meadows of the wood.

7 We will arise, and to his tents
    and tabernacles go:
  we will him worship, and with joy
    bow at his footstool low.

8 Arise, O Lord, into the place
    wherein thy rest shall be;
  arise do thou, yea, and the ark
    of thine own strength with thee.

9 O let thy priests, unto thee nigh,
    be clothed with righteousness;
  and let thy saints about thee round
    shout loud for joyfulness.

10 For thine own servant David's sake
    no more do thou delay:
  the face of thine anointed one
    turn not from thee away.

11 The Lord in truth to David sware,
    and will not it deny,
  Of fruit of thine own body set
    upon thy throne will I.

12 If thy seed will my cov'nant keep,
    and testimony sure,
  that I'll them teach, sit on thy throne
    their seed shall evermore.

13 For, lo, of Zion hath the Lord
    made choice assuredly;
  he hath desired it, that it should
    his habitation be.

14 This is my rest for evermore,
    saith he, here will I dwell;
  it is the place that I've desired,
    for I do like it well.

15 Her bounty and provision bless
    abundantly will I:
her poor and needy I with bread
    will daily satisfy.

16 I also with salvation sure
    her priests will clothe about:
moreover those that are her saints
    for joy aloud shall shout.

17 The horn of David there to bud
    in faithfulness I'll make:
I also have ordained a lamp
    for mine anointed's sake.

18 I will his en'mies clothe with shame,
    and all his foes cast down:
but on himself in majesty
    shall flourish long his crown.

PSALM 133

A Song of degrees of David

Lydia

1 BEHOLD, how good, how pleasing well,
    for such as brethren be
to dwell together, and as one
    to join in unity!

2 'Tis like the good oil on the head,
    that down the beard did flow,
e'en Aaron's beard, that to the fringe
    did of his garments go:

3 As Hermon's dew, the dew that did
    on Zion's mounts descend:
for there the LORD the blessing charged,
    life that shall never end.

Psalm 134

A Song of degrees

Repton

1 BEHOLD, bless ye the LORD, all ye
 the servants of the LORD,
which do within the LORD's house stand
 by night with one accord.
2 Your hands lift in the sanctuary,
 and bless the LORD do ye.
3 The LORD that heav'n and earth did make
 from Zion hill bless thee.

Psalm 135

Evangel

1 PRAISE ye the LORD. The LORD's great name
 praise ye with one accord;
O do ye render praise to him,
 ye servants of the LORD.
2 Ye in the LORD's house that do stand,
 his service to fulfil,
that in the courts of our God's house
 do stand to serve him still,

3 The LORD praise; for the LORD is good:
 O do ye praises sing
unto his name; because it is
 a good and pleasant thing.
4 Of Jacob hath the LORD made choice,
 that he might with him dwell;
for his peculiar treasure he
 hath chosen Israel.

5 For I know that the LORD is great,
   and over all abides;
and that our Lord is far above
   all other gods besides.

6 For whatsoever pleased the LORD
   he did in heaven high,
in earth, the seas, and places all
   within the deep that lie.

7 The vapours causeth he to rise
   from ends of earth that be;
he lightnings makes for rain; the wind
   from treasuries brings he.

8 Who smote the first-born to the ground
   that did in Egypt dwell;
of man and beast not one was spared,
   alike he did them fell.

9 Who tokens did with wonders send,
   that in thy midst did fall,
O Egypt, which on Pharaoh came,
   and on his servants all.

10 Who great and famous nations smote,
   and kings most mighty slew;

11 Sihon, king of the Amorites,
   Og, king of Bashan, too;

And Canaan's kingdoms all he smote:
12   for heritage gave he
their land to Isr'el; heritage
   that should his people's be.

13 O LORD, thy name assuredly
   endure for ever shall;
and thy memorial, O LORD,
   through generations all.

14 For judge his people will the LORD
    with truth and equity;
concerning those that do him serve
    repent himself will he.

15 Of silver and of gold are made
    the heathen's idols all:
the work they be of those men's hands
    that down before them fall.

16 Mouths have they, but they do not speak;
    eyes, but they do not see;
17 ears, but hear not; nor in their mouths
    can any breathing be.
18 Behold, like unto them are those
    that with their hands them frame:
and so is every one that doth
    his trust place in the same.

19 O house of Isr'el, bless the LORD:
    and bless the LORD, all ye
20 of Aaron's house: bless ye the LORD,
    of Levi's house that be:
Bless ye the LORD, that fear the LORD.
21   From Zion blessed be
the LORD which at Jerus'lem dwells.
    Praise to the LORD give ye.

PSALM 136

Forest Green

1 O GIVE thanks to the LORD: 'tis good;
    his mercy doth endure.
2 O give thanks to the God of gods:
    endures his mercy sure.

3 O give thanks to the Lord of lords:
   his mercy doth endure.
4 To him who worketh wonders great:
   endures his mercy sure.

5 To him that heav'ns by wisdom made:
   his mercy doth endure.
6 To him that earth 'bove waters stretched:
   endures his mercy sure.
7 To him that made great lights above:
   his mercy doth endure:
8 the sun to rule throughout the day:
   endures his mercy sure:

9 The moon and stars to rule by night:
   his mercy doth endure.
10 To him that Egypt's first-born smote:
   endures his mercy sure:
11 And Isr'el from their midst brought out:
   his mercy doth endure:
12 with strength of hand and stretched-out arm:
   endures his mercy sure.

13 To him which did the Red sea part:
   his mercy doth endure:
14 and through its midst made Isr'el pass:
   endures his mercy sure:
15 But did of Pharaoh and his host
   the overthrow assure,
   and in the Red sea did them drown:
   his mercy doth endure.

16 To him which did his people lead
   and made them to endure
   throughout the barren wilderness:
   endures his mercy sure.

17 To him which smote great kings and strong:
　　his mercy doth endure:
18 and slew moreover famous kings:
　　endures his mercy sure:
19 Yea, Sihon of the Am'rites king:
　　his mercy doth endure:
20 and Og which was of Bashan king:
　　endures his mercy sure:
21 And gave their land an heritage:
　　his mercy doth endure:
22 and made his servant Isr'el heir:
　　endures his mercy sure.

23 Who us in low estate did mind:
　　his mercy doth endure:
24 and hath redeemed us from our foes:
　　endures his mercy sure.
25 Who unto all flesh giveth food:
　　his mercy doth endure.
26 O give thanks to the God of heaven:
　　endures his mercy sure.

PSALM 137

Rest

1 BY river-sides of Babylon
　　　we sat down, yea, we wept,
　when Zion we did call to mind
　　　that there were captive kept.
2 In midst thereof we hanged our harps
　　the willow-trees along:
3 for they that captive carried us
　　required of us a song;

　And they that wasted us required
　　that to them mirth we bring,

290

and said, Now one of Zion's songs
    do ye unto us sing.
4 How in a strange land shall we sing
5   the LORD's song? if I thee
forget, Jerus'lem, let forgone
    my right hand's cunning be.

6 If thee I mind not, let my tongue
    to my mouth's roof cleave fast;
if that Jerus'lem hath not far
    my chiefest joy surpassed.

7 Remember Edom's children, LORD,
    who in Jerus'lem's day,
To its foundation raze it down,
    yea, raze it down, did say.

8 O daughter thou of Babylon,
    who art destroyed to be;
he happy is, as thou'st served us,
    that thus rewardeth thee.

9 Yea, happy shall he be that doth
    take up thy little ones,
as thou didst ours, and cast them down
    to dash against the stones.

PSALM 138

A Psalm of David

Bishopthorpe

1 I WILL thee praise with my whole heart:
    sing praise to thee will I
2 before the gods, and worship t'ward
    thy holy temple high.
For loving-kindness thine, and truth,
    thy name I'll praise and laud:

because thou over all thy name
    hast magnified thy word.

3 Thou answeredst me in the day
    when I did cry to thee,
and strengthenedst me in my soul
    with strength abundantly.
4 The kings and rulers all, O LORD,
    upon the earth that live,
when they the words hear of thy mouth
    shall praise unto thee give.

5 Yea, in the LORD's ways they shall all
    sing forth with one accord;
for great appeareth unto them
    the glory of the LORD.
6 Although the LORD be high, yet still
    to those that lowly be
he hath respect: whereas the proud
    afar off knoweth he.

7 Though I in midst of trouble walk,
    thou wilt me cause to live:
thine hand shall stretch 'gainst my foes' wrath,
    thy right hand safety give.
8 That which concerns me will the LORD
    make perfect: ever stands
thy mercy, LORD: forsake thou not
    the works of thine own hands.

PSALM 139

To the chief Musician, A Psalm of David.

Hermon

1 LORD, thou'st me searched and known: and
2   my sitting down dost see,   (thou

and rising up: my thought far off
  is understood by thee.
3 My pathway, and my lying down,
    thou compassest always,
  and e'en acquainted perfectly
    art thou with all my ways.

4 For there is not a single word
    that in my tongue doth dwell,
  but, lo, O Lord, thou dost it know,
    and altogether tell.
5 Behind me, and before my face,
    thou hast me round beset;
  thou hast my goings marked, and thou
    thine hand hast on me set.

6 Such knowledge is too wonderful,
    too much for me to gain;
  so high it is, that unto it
    I cannot once attain.
7 Where from thy spirit shall I go?
    where from thy presence hide?
8 If I ascend up into heaven,
    then there thou dost abide:

  And if I make my bed in hell,
    behold, there thou shalt be:
9 take I the wings of morn and dwell
    in utmost parts of sea,
10 Me even there thy hand shall lead,
    and shall my way unfold;
  yea, verily, I know in truth,
    thy right hand shall me hold.

11 If I should say, The darkness deep
    shall surely cover me,
  then shall the very night itself
    as light about me be.
12 Yea, darkness from thee hideth not,
    but night doth shine as day:
  to thee the darkness and the light
    are both alike alway.

13 For thou hast long possessed my reins,
    and thou hast covered me
  when laid within my mother's womb:
14   I will give praise to thee.
  For fearfully and wonderfully
    thou didst my being frame:
  thy works are marv'llous; and my soul
    right well doth know the same.

15 My substance, when in secret made,
    was hidden not from thee,
  when I within earth's lowest parts
    was wrought most curiously.
16 Yet being unperfect, thine eyes
    did on my substance look;
  and of my members every one
    was written in thy book;

  Which in their due continuance
    were fashioned, when of old
  as yet there was not one of them,
    and none them to behold.
17 How precious also are the thoughts
    thou hast, O God, to me!
  and in the sum of them how great
    and numberless they be!

18 If I should count them, they are more
    in number than the sand:
when I awake from sleep, I still
    am with thee close at hand.

19 All those that do work wickedness
    thou'lt surely slay, O God:
depart ye therefore far from me,
    ye bloody men abhorred.

20 For they against thee wickedly
    speak forth with words profane,
and those that are thine enemies
    do take thy name in vain.

21 Do not I hate all them, O LORD,
    that hatred bear to thee?
and am I not much grieved with those
    that risen 'gainst thee be?

22 With perfect hatred them I hate,
    accounting each a foe.

23 Search me, O God, and know my heart:
    me try, my thoughts to know:

24 And see if any wicked way
    within me there should be;
and in the everlasting way
    give guidance unto me.

PSALM 140

To the chief Musician, A Psalm of David.

S. Fulbert

1 O LORD, safe from the evil man
    do thou deliver me:
and from the man of violence
    preserve and keep me free;

2 Which do imagine mischiefs ill
   within their heart alway;
together gathered as for war
   continually are they.

3 Their tongues they cruelly sharpened have
   like to a serpent's tongue;
beneath their lips is poison which
   to adders doth belong.

4 LORD, keep me from the wicked's hands;
   and from the violent foe
preserve me; for my goings they
   have purposed to o'erthrow.

5 The proud for me a snare have hid,
   and cords; and they a net
have likewise by the wayside spread:
   they gins for me have set.

6 Then to the LORD thus did I speak,
   Behold, thou art my God:
unto my supplications' voice
   do thou give ear, O LORD.

7 O GOD the Lord, who art the strength
   of my salvation sure,
thou for the battle covered hast
   my head in time of war.

8 The wicked man's desires grant not,
   O LORD, when he doth pray:
nor further thou his ill device;
   lest vaunt themselves do they.

9 As for the head of those that do
   encompass me around,
let of their lips the mischief great
   them cover and confound.

10 Let burning coals upon them fall:
   let them be cast straightway
into the fire; into deep pits,
   that rise no more may they.

11 Let not established in the earth
   an evil speaker be:
for evil shall the violent hunt
   and cast down utterly.

12 I know that the afflicted's cause
   the LORD maintaineth still,
and that uphold continually
   the poor man's right he will.

13 The righteous surely shall give thanks
   unto thy name always:
and in thy presence upright men
   shall dwell throughout their days.

PSALM 141

A Psalm of David

S. Peter

1 O LORD, I unto thee cry out:
   do thou make haste to me;
give ear unto my voice, I pray,
   when I cry unto thee.

2 Set forth before thee let my prayer
   as incense sweet arise;
the lifting of mine hands just as
   the evening sacrifice.

3 Set, LORD, a watch before my mouth;
   keep of my lips the door:

4 my heart to any evil thing
   let be inclined no more;

297

With men that work iniquity,
    let not, I thee entreat,
me practise wicked works: nor let
    me of their dainties eat.

5 Let him that righteous is me smite;
    it shall a kindness be:
let him reprove me; it shall seem
    oil excellent to me,
Which shall not break my head: for yet
    the prayer that I shall make
shall be when such calamities
    them also overtake.

6 What time their judges overthrown
    in stony places be,
then shall they likewise hear the words
    that sweet have been to me.

7 About the entrance of the grave
    our bones are scattered round,
as wood which one doth cut and cleave
    lies strewn upon the ground.

8 But unto thee, O God the Lord,
    mine eyes are lifted high:
my soul leave thou not destitute,
    for in thee trust do I.

9 Preserve me from the hidden snares
    which they have laid for me,
and from the secret gins of those
    that work iniquity.

10 The wicked into their own nets
    let fall, and fast be caught;
what time that I escape withal,
    and am to safety brought.

PSALM 142

Maschil of David;
A Prayer when he was in the cave.

Culross

1   I TO the LORD cried with my voice,
        and in my trouble spake;
    I to the LORD did with my voice
        my supplication make.

2   Before him I my sore complaint
        poured out in my distress;
    before him I my trouble showed,
        and did my grief express.

3   When overwhelmed my spirit was,
        and brought within me low,
    when I was in perplexity,
        then thou my path didst know.
    For in the way wherein I walked
        I did the wicked see,
    which privily in counsel joined
        to lay a snare for me.

4   I to my right looked, and beheld,
        but no man knew me there;
    all refuge failed me: for my soul
        there was no man to care.

5   LORD, I did cry: I said, Thou art
        a refuge unto me;
    thou art my portion in the land
        of those that living be.

6   Because I am brought very low,
        attend unto my cry:
    me from my persecutors free
        that stronger are than I.

299

7 That I may praise thy name, my soul
    from prison set thou free:
the just me compass shall; for thou'lt
    deal bountif'lly with me.

PSALM 143

A Psalm of David

Elgin

1 MY prayer, LORD, and entreaties hear:
    in thy great faithfulness
give thou an answer unto me,
    and in thy righteousness.

2 And into judgment bring thou not
    thy servant to be tried:
because no living man shall be
    in thy sight justified.

3 The en'my persecuted hath
    and vexed my soul with strife;
moreover he unto the ground
    hath smitten down my life;
He hath in darkness made me dwell,
    as those long dead that be:

4 my spirit's overwhelmed; my heart
    is desolate in me.

5 I call to mind the days of old;
    upon thy works each one
I meditate; and muse on all
    the work thy hands have done.

6 I unto thee stretch forth my hands:
    my soul doth thirst for thee,
as in a dry and thirsty land
    wherein no waters be.

7 LORD, hear with speed: my spirit fails:
　　hide not thy face from me,
　lest like unto them that go down
　　into the pit I be.
8 Cause that thy loving-kindness shall
　　me in the morning wake;
　for thee I trust: cause me to know
　　the way that I should take;

　For I to thee lift up my soul.
9　　LORD, do thou set me free
　from all my foes: me safely hide,
　　for unto thee I flee.
10 Because thou art my God, me teach
　　to do thy will indeed:
　good is thy spirit, to the land
　　of uprightness me lead.

11 For thy name's sake, O LORD, do thou
　　me quicken and make whole:
　because of thine own righteousness
　　from trouble bring my soul.
12 And of thy mercy cut off those
　　that en'mies are to me;
　destroy them all that vex my soul:
　　I servant am to thee.

PSALM 144

A Psalm of David

S. Matthew

1 FOR ever blessed be the LORD,
　　who is my strength and might;
　who doth direct my hands to war,
　　my fingers teach to fight:

2 My goodness, fortress; my high tower,
    he that doth set me free;
my shield, my trust; who doth subdue
    my people under me.

3 LORD, what is man, that ever thou
    of him dost knowledge take!
or what the son of man, that thou
    of him account dost make!

4 Man is but vain; as shadows pass,
    his days do swiftly end.

5 Do thou, O LORD, thy heavens bow:
    unto the earth descend;

    The mountains touch, and they shall smoke:
6   cast forth thy lightning bright;
them scatter: shoot thine arrows out;
    destroy them by thy might.

7 Do thou thine hand send from above;
    rid and deliver me
out of great waters, from the hand
    of children strange that be;

8 Whose mouth doth utter vanity,
    and speak forth with conceit;
and their right hand a right hand is
    of falsehood and deceit.

9 A new song I will sing, O God,
    upon a psaltery,
and on a ten-stringed instrument
    I'll praises sing to thee.

10 For he it is that unto kings
    salvation doth afford:
who doth his servant David keep
    safe from the hurtful sword.

11 Rid, free me from strange children's hand,
    whose mouth speaks vanity,
and their right hand a right hand is
    of falsehood unto me:

12 That in their youth our sons as plants
    may grow; our daughters fair
as polished corner-stones, that to
    a palace may compare:

13 That full our garners be, of store
    all manner to afford:
that our sheep thousands, thousands ten,
    bear in our streets abroad:

14 That strong our oxen be to toil;
    that no in-breaking be,
nor going out; and that our streets
    be of complaining free.

15 O blessed be that people all
    in such a case as this:
bless'd be that people all, whose God
    the LORD most surely is.

PSALM 145

David's Psalm of praise

Denfield

1 I'LL thee extol, my God, O king;
    and I will bless thy name:
for ever and for ever I
    will surely bless the same.

2 Each day I will thee gladly bless;
    and I will praise thy name:
for ever and for ever I
    will surely praise the same.

3 Great is the LORD, and to be praised
    exceedingly is he;
  and of his greatness infinite
    no searching there can be.
4 One generation shall thy works
    unto another praise;
  and shall declare thy mighty deeds,
    thine acts of former days.

5 I of the glorious honour will
    speak of thy majesty,
  and of the works which thou hast wrought
    that great and wondrous be.
6 And of thine acts most terrible
    shall men speak of the might:
  and to declare thy greatness I
    will also take delight.

7 Abundantly they shall each day
    the memory express
  of all thy goodness great, and shall
    sing of thy righteousness.
8 The LORD is gracious in his ways,
    and of compassion full;
  to anger slow, of mercy great,
    in kindness plentiful.

9 The LORD his goodness doth bestow
    on all, both near and far;
  and over all his handiworks
    his tender mercies are.
10 Thee all thy works shall praise, O LORD,
    and thee thy saints shall bless.
11 They'll of thy kingdom's glory speak,
    and shall thy pow'r confess;

12 To make known to men's sons his acts
    that great and mighty be,
and of his kingdom excellent
    the glorious majesty.
13 Thy kingdom everlasting is,
    thy kingdom doth endure;
and thy dominion stands throughout
    all generations sure.

14 The LORD upholdeth all that fall,
    the bowed he lifts anew.
15 All eyes wait on thee; them their meat
    thou giv'st in season due.
16 For thou dost open wide thine hand,
    and bounty forth doth spring:
thou satisfiest the desire
    of every living thing.

17 The LORD is righteous in his ways,
    and in his paths each one;
he holy is in all the works
    that by his hands are done.
18 To all that on him call the LORD
    found nigh at hand shall be,
to all that do upon him call
    in truth and verity.

19 He will the just desire fulfil
    of them that do him fear:
he'll also hear their cry, and he
    to save them will appear.
20 Each one that beareth love to him
    the LORD preserveth still:
but workers all of wickedness
    destroy in wrath he will.

21 My mouth the praise shall of the LORD
  with joyfulness proclaim:
and let all flesh for ever bless
  his great and holy name.

PSALM 146

Palestrina

1 PRAISE ye the LORD. O render praise
  unto the LORD, my soul.
2 I while I live will praise the LORD,
  and gladly him extol;
While I have breath, unto my God
  in praises sing will I,
yea, while I any being have
  I will him magnify.

3 In princes put ye not your trust,
  on them for aid to call;
nor in the son of man, in whom
  there is no help at all.
4 His breath goes forth, he to his earth
  returneth to decay;
then perish all his inmost thoughts
  within that very day.

5 He happy is that Jacob's God
  hath for his help and aid,
he in the LORD his God whose hope
  and confidence is stayed:
6 Which did the heaven make, and earth,
  the sea, and swelling deep,
with all that doth therein abide:
  which truth doth ever keep:

7 Which executeth judgment just
    for those oppressed that be:
which to the hungry giveth food.
    The LORD sets pris'ners free:
8 The LORD blind eyes doth open wide:
    the LORD the bowed doth raise:
the LORD doth love the righteous well,
    and those of upright ways:

9 The LORD the strangers doth preserve;
    orphans and widows he
relieveth: but the wicked's way
    turned upside-down shall be.
10 The LORD shall reign for evermore;
    thy God, O Zion, he
to generations all doth reign.
    Praise to the LORD give ye.

PSALM 147

Dunfermline

1 PRAISE ye the LORD: for it is good
    psalms to our God to sing;
for it is pleasant; and to praise
    it is a comely thing.
2 The LORD builds up Jerusalem:
    and he it is alone
that Isr'el's outcasts gathereth
    together into one.

3 The broken-hearted he doth heal,
    their wounds he binds withal.
4 He tells the number of the stars,
    by name he calls them all.

5 Great is our Lord, and of great power:
   his wisdom hath no bound.
6 The LORD lifts up the meek, and casts
   the wicked to the ground.

7 O come, and with thanksgiving sing
   in songs unto the LORD;
   upon the harp with pleasant sound
   sing praise unto our God:
8 Who heaven covereth with clouds,
   who for the earth below
   prepareth rain, who maketh grass
   upon the mountains grow.

9 He gives the beast his food, and feeds
   the ravens young which cry.
10 He no delight takes in the strength
   that in the horse doth lie;
   He gains no pleasure from man's legs.
11 The LORD doth pleasure gain
   from them that fear him, and that hope
   his mercy to obtain.

12 The LORD praise, O Jerusalem;
   thy God, O Zion, praise:
13 for of thy gates he hath with might
   made strong the bars and stays;
   Thy children in thee he hath bless'd.
14 Thy peace he makes complete
   in all thy coasts, and fills thee with
   the finest of the wheat.

15 He his commandment sendeth forth
   upon the earth: his word
16 runs very swiftly: he gives snow
   like wool dispersed abroad:

And he the hoar-frost scattereth
    like ashes manifold:
17 like morsels casts he forth his ice:
    who can withstand his cold?

18 His word he sendeth, and them melts:
    he makes his wind to blow
and doth dispel the cold so that
    the waters freely flow.
19 His holy word and doctrine he
    doth unto Jacob tell:
his statutes and his judgments just
    he shows to Israel.

20 With any nation on this wise
    not dealt at all hath he:
his judgments they have never known.
    Praise to the LORD give ye.

PSALM 148

Glasgow

1 PRAISE ye the LORD. From heavens high
    praise to the LORD give ye:
and to him render praise throughout
    the heights above that be.
2 All ye his angels, praise ye him:
    praise him, all hosts of might.
3 Praise him, ye sun and moon: him praise,
    O all ye stars of light.

4 Praise him, ye highest heavens which
    he o'er the heav'ns did raise,
and waters far above the heavens;
5   the LORD's name let them praise:

For they created were and formed,
    what time commanded he:
6 he hath for ever stablished them,
    and made a fixed decree.

7 Ye dragons, and all places deep,
    from earth praise ye the LORD:
8 fire, hail, snow, vapour, stormy wind,
    fulfilling all his word:
9 High mountains, and all hills that rise;
    trees fruitful, cedars all:
10 beasts, and all cattle; creeping things,
    and flying fowl withal:

11 Kings of the earth, all people known;
    princes, earth's judges all:
12 both men of youth, and maidens fair;
    old men, and children small:
13 The LORD's name let them praise: his name
    is excellent alone;
above the earth and heaven high
    his glory is made known.

14 His people's horn, all his saints' praise,
    withal exalteth he;
of Isr'el's sons, a people near
    to him. The LORD praise ye.

PSALM 149

Amazing Grace

1 PRAISE ye the LORD. O do ye sing
    a new song to the LORD,
and in the meeting of the saints
    his praise do ye record.

2 In him that did him being give
    let Isr'el joy and sing:
let Zion's children every one
    be joyful in their King.

3 And let them praise him in the dance,
    his name to magnify:
let them with timbrel and with harp
    sing praises sounding high.

4 The LORD doth pleasure take in those
    that his own people be:
with his salvation beautify
    those that are meek will he.

5 In glory also let the saints
    with joyfulness delight:
let them with gladness sing aloud
    upon their beds at night.

6 The praises high that God exalt
    let in their mouth abound:
and let a sharp and two-edged sword
    within their hand be found;

7 To execute the vengeance due
    upon the heathen all,
and on the people punishments
    with justice make to fall;

8 Their kings that ruled in majesty
    with heavy chains to bind;
their nobles too, that they might be
    with iron bands confined:

9 To execute upon each one
    the written judgment word:
this honour great have all his saints.
    O do ye praise the LORD.

Psalm 150

Lyngham

1 PRAISE ye the Lord. Give praise to God
within his sanctuary:
O praise him in the firmament
of his great power do ye.

2 Praise him for all his mighty acts:
him praise with solemn sound
according as his greatness doth
in excellence abound.

3 Praise him with trumpet's sound: his praise
with psaltery advance,

4 and with the harp: give praise to him
with timbrel and the dance:
His praise with all stringed instruments
and organs magnify:

5 praise him on cymbals loud: him praise
on cymbals sounding high.

6 Let every creature praise the Lord,
yea, all that living be,
and every thing that hath his breath.
Praise to the Lord give ye.

THE END OF THE PSALMS

Index of First Lines

In thee, O LORD, I put my trust;	31
In thee, O LORD, I put my trust:	71
In thy great wrath, I thee beseech,	38
In Zion praise doth wait, O God,	65
Incline and hear the right, O LORD,	17

Judge me, and plead my cause against	43

Let God arise: his enemies	68
LORD God of my salvation, hear:	88
LORD, thou art he that favourable	85
LORD, thou art just: upright appear	119 (18)
Lord, thou hast been our dwelling-place,	90
LORD, thou'st me searched and known: and thou	139

Make to the LORD a joyful noise,	100
Many a time afflicted me	129
Me hear, God of my righteousness,	4
My God, from all mine enemies	59
My God, my God, why hast thou me	22
My heart is fixed, O God, I'll sing;	108
My heart not haughty is, O LORD,	131
My portion and inheritance	119 (8)
My prayer, LORD, and entreaties hear:	143
My soul expecting all day long	62
My soul for thy salvation faints:	119 (11)
My soul, the LORD bless: LORD my God,	104
My soul unto the dust doth cleave	119 (4)
My voice, O God, hear in my prayer,	64

Not unto us, LORD, not to us,	115

O blessed are the undefiled	119 (1)
O clap your hands, ye people all,	47
O come, and let us to the LORD	95
O congregation, do ye speak	58

Selected Verses for Singing

322

N.B. *Where the space allowed under the heading 'verses' is left blank in the table above, the whole psalm is to be sung.*

Sources of Recommended Tunes

1 The tune named at the head of each psalm is recommended for use with that psalm. The tunes have been chosen with great care and are mostly traditional psalm tunes, though some newer tunes have also been included.

2 No tune has been used more than twice throughout the whole psalter, and some tunes occur only once. Rarely, therefore, should two psalms with an identical tune be chosen in one and the same meeting. However, should this occur, the discretion of the precentor must be exercised as to the selection of an alternative tune.

3 Sometimes different parts of a psalm are diverse in character, especially in the case of the longer compositions. In such instances we have chosen a tune which suits what appears to be the predominant tenor of the whole psalm. Nevertheless, when an integral section from that psalm is to be sung, having its own distinctive character, then we suggest that the precentor exercises suitable initiative in the choice of a tune. As an instance of this, in Psalm 89 the overall tune Noel might be considered insufficiently solemn for singing the selected section of verses 47-52: in such a case the precentor would choose at his discretion, say, Dundee, or Culross, as an alternative.

4 With the exception of the common metre tune Grafton, all the suggested tunes may be found in the following books:

The Methodist Hymn Book (35th Edition 1972)
Hymns of Faith (1964)
The Church Hymnary (April 1927)
Companion Tune Book (6th Edition) to Gadsby's Hymn Book

Second Supplement to Companion Tune Book (1974)
The Scottish Psalmody (Free Church of Scotland) (sol-fa Edition 1977)
Hymns for Today's Church (1st Edition 1982)
Christian Hymns (1st Edition 1977) (Evangelical Movement of Wales)
Sacred Songs and Solos (Sankey's) (1200 tune edition)
The Scottish Psalter (1929) (staff edition)

5 In some cases an identical tune may appear under a different name in another tune-book: where this occurs, the alternative name is given in brackets in the following table. Again, different books render the same basic tune in varying forms: in that case we have referred to the form of the tune considered to be most appropriate for the singing of the psalms.

6 Unless indicated in the following table as short metre (SM), double common metre (DCM) or double short metre (DSM), all the tunes are straightforward common metre, with the exception of those few tunes which have repeating lines. For instance, with Repton, although basically a common metre tune, both the third and fourth lines are repeated in each verse.

7 Occasionally a double common metre tune (which of necessity requires an even number of verses for singing) has been set to a psalm of which the sum of the verses is an odd number. In that case one of the verses must be repeated. An appropriate suggestion has been carefully chosen to meet this contingency. The repeat verse has been clearly indicated at the conclusion of the psalm.

Name of Tune	Source of Tune	No.
Abbey	Methodist Hymn Book (35th Ed. 1972)	698
Abney	Hymns of Faith (1964)	184
Amazing Grace	Hymns of Faith (1964)	50 (i)
Argyle	The Scottish Psalmody (Free Church of Scotland) (sol-fa Ed. 1977)	22
Arnold (Arnold's)	Companion Tune Book (6th Ed.)	91

★

Ballerma	Methodist Hymn Book (35th Ed. 1972)	559
Bangor	The Church Hymnary (April 1927)	313 (i)
Barrow	The Scottish Psalmody (Free Church of Scotland) (sol-fa Ed. 1977)	30
Beatitudo	Methodist Hymn Book (35th Ed. 1972)	604 (ii)
Belmont	Methodist Hymn Book (35th Ed. 1972)	766
Bishopthorpe	Methodist Hymn Book (35th Ed. 1972)	107
Bristol	Methodist Hymn Book (35th Ed. 1972)	82
Brother James' Air	Hymns for Today's Church (1st Ed. 1982)	591 (ii)

★

Caithness	The Church Hymnary (April 1927)	481 (i)
Calvary (SM) (without refrain)	Methodist Hymn Book (35th Ed. 1972)	351
Caroline	The Scottish Psalter (1929) (staff edition)	38
Colchester	The Church Hymnary (April 1927) Supplement	732
Coleshill	Methodist Hymn Book (35th Ed. 1972)	464
Crediton	Methodist Hymn Book (35th Ed. 1972)	565
Crimond	Companion Tune Book (6th Ed.) Supplement	851
Culross	The Church Hymnary (April 1927)	353 (i)

★

Dalehurst	Hymns of Faith (1964)	121 (i)

329

Name of Tune	Source of Tune	No.
Denfield	Companion Tune Book (6th Ed.)	127
Drumclog	The Scottish Psalter (1929) (staff edition)	49
Dundee (Windsor)	Methodist Hymn Book (35th Ed. 1972)	237
Dunfermline	Methodist Hymn Book (35th Ed. 1972)	37

★

Effingham	Second Supplement to Companion Tune Book (1974)	923
Elgin	The Church Hymnary (April 1927)	246 (i)
Ellacombe (DCM)	Companion Tune Book (6th Ed.)	267
Evan	Hymns of Faith (1964)	261
Evangel (DCM)	The Church Hymnary (April 1927)	42

★

Forest Green (DCM)	Methodist Hymn Book (35th Ed. 1972)	897
French (Dundee)	Methodist Hymn Book (35th Ed. 1972)	625

★

Glasgow	Methodist Hymn Book (35th Ed. 1972)	904
Gloucester	The Church Hymnary (April 1927)	223 (ii)
Gräfenberg	The Scottish Psalmody (Free Church of Scotland) (sol-fa Ed. 1977)	70
Grafton	(source unknown) (American composer: Lowell Mason, Mus.D.)	

★

Harington	Methodist Hymn Book (35th Ed. 1972)	413
Hermon	The Scottish Psalmody (Free Church of Scotland) (sol-fa Ed. 1977)	74
Horsley	Methodist Hymn Book (35th Ed. 1972)	180

★

Jackson (Byzantium) (Jackson's)	Methodist Hymn Book (35th Ed. 1972)	342

★

Name of Tune	Source of Tune	No.
Kedron	Christian Hymns (1st Ed. 1977)	368
Kilmarnock	Methodist Hymn Book (35th Ed. 1972)	50
Kilsyth	The Scottish Psalter (1929) (staff edition)	76
Kingsfold (DCM)	Methodist Hymn Book (35th Ed. 1972)	154 (i)

★

Lloyd	Methodist Hymn Book (35th Ed. 1972) Additional Tunes	(AT)29
London New (London)	Methodist Hymn Book (35th Ed. 1972)	224
Lydia	Methodist Hymn Book (35th Ed. 1972)	1 (ii)
Lyngham (Nativity)	Hymns of Faith (1964)	1 (ii)
Lynton	Methodist Hymn Book (35th Ed. 1972)	442

★

Martyrdom	Methodist Hymn Book (35th Ed. 1972)	201
Martyrs (Old Martyrs)	The Church Hymnary (April 1927)	520
Moravia	The Church Hymnary (April 1927)	306
Morven	The Church Hymnary (April 1927) Supplement	770 (ii)

★

Nearer Home (DSM)	Methodist Hymn Book (35th Ed. 1972)	658
Newington (S. Stephen)	Methodist Hymn Book (35th Ed. 1972)	56
Noel (DCM)	Methodist Hymn Book (35th Ed. 1972)	130

★

Old 18th (DCM)	The Church Hymnary (April 1927)	586 (ii)
Old 22nd (DCM)	The Church Hymnary (April 1927)	486
Old 81st (DCM)	The Church Hymnary (April 1927)	355 (i)

★

Palestrina	The Church Hymnary (April 1927) Supplement	773

331

Name of Tune	Source of Tune	No.
Petersham (DCM)	The Church Hymnary (April 1927)	398

★

Redhead No. 66 (Waveney)	Methodist Hymn Book (35th Ed. 1972)	160
Repton	Hymns of Faith (1964)	95 (ii)
Rest	Methodist Hymn Book (35th Ed. 1972) Additional Tunes	(AT) 23

★

S. Agnes	Methodist Hymn Book (35th Ed. 1972)	289
S. Anne (Ann's)	Methodist Hymn Book (35th Ed. 1972)	878
S. Bernard	Methodist Hymn Book (35th Ed. 1972)	408
S. Bride (SM)	Methodist Hymn Book (35th Ed. 1972)	81
S. Columba (Erin)	Methodist Hymn Book (35th Ed. 1972)	51
S. David	Methodist Hymn Book (35th Ed. 1972)	721
S. Flavian	Methodist Hymn Book (35th Ed. 1972)	43
S. Frances	Methodist Hymn Book (35th Ed. 1972)	454
S. Fulbert	Methodist Hymn Book (35th Ed. 1972)	604 (i)
S. James	Methodist Hymn Book (35th Ed. 1972)	307
S. Kilda	The Church Hymnary (April 1927)	558 (i)
S. Magnus (Nottingham)	The Church Hymnary (April 1927)	131
S. Mary	Methodist Hymn Book (35th Ed. 1972)	175
S. Matthew (DCM)	Methodist Hymn Book (35th Ed. 1972)	824
S. Peter	Methodist Hymn Book (35th Ed. 1972)	99
S. Stephen (Abridge)	Methodist Hymn Book (35th Ed. 1972)	519
Salzburg	The Church Hymnary (April 1927)	562 (i)
Sawley	Methodist Hymn Book (35th Ed. 1972) Additional Tunes	(AT) 9
Selma (SM)	Methodist Hymn Book (35th Ed. 1972)	54

Name of Tune	Source of Tune	No.
Sheffield (Attercliffe)	Methodist Hymn Book (35th Ed. 1972)	333
Spohr	The Church Hymnary (April 1927)	451 (i)
Stracathro	Methodist Hymn Book (35th Ed. 1972)	102
Stroudwater	The Church Hymnary (April 1927) Supplement	747 (i)

★

Tallis (Tallis' Ordinal)	Methodist Hymn Book (35th Ed. 1972)	304
There is a Fountain (with refrain DCM)	Sacred Songs and Solos	129
Tiverton	The Church Hymnary (April 1927)	57

★

Vox Dilecti (DCM)	Methodist Hymn Book (35th Ed. 1972)	154 (ii)

★

Westminster	Methodist Hymn Book (35th Ed. 1972)	73
Wigtown	Methodist Hymn Book (35th Ed. 1972)	512
Wiltshire	The Church Hymnary (April 1927) Supplement	735
Winchester (Winchester Old)	Methodist Hymn Book (35th Ed. 1972)	129

★

York	Methodist Hymn Book (35th Ed. 1972)	347